Joe Pauker

GET LOST!

The Cool Guide to Amsterdam

D0066829

Get Lost Publishing

June 2001

British Library in Publication Data. A catalogue record for this book is available from the British Library.

© Get Lost Publishing, June 2001

ISBN: 90-76499-01-2

For all their help, advice, information, and support, many thanks to...
Aaron, American Book Center, Amsterdam Call Girls, Annie, Anthony, Brian, Candy, Christian & Ann, Claudia, Clyde, Curt & Nancy, Dave & Dian, Ellen, Gaëlle, George, The Headshop, Hemp Hotel, Kay, Klaus, Kokopelli, Michel, Mom, Monica, Mor & Fred, Pip, Pop, Richard & Elard, Richard, Rick, Roland, Rosa & Art, Roy, Sagarmatha Seeds, Sensi Seed Bank, Steve, Susan, Tess & Rene, Uln, Walter, Yuri... and most of all, Lisa.

Editing and research assistance by **Lisa Kristensen**

Cover design by **Ellen Pauker**

Photos by **Joe Pauker**

Printed in Amsterdam with vegetable-based inks on 100% post-consumer-waste recycled paper.

QUESTION
AUTHORITY

INTRODUCTION

Congratulations! You're in the most happening city in Europe and you've got a copy of *Get Lost!* Inside, you'll find the things that I look for when I visit a new city: cool, underground places that often aren't found in other guides, plus all the practical information I need to find my way around easily and quickly. I wrote the first edition of *The Cool Guide* during a period when I didn't have a TV. I borrowed a friend's computer, and spent a week typing up my hand-written manuscript. When I returned the computer (this is a true story), my friend plugged it in and it blew up! I distributed that edition using only my bicycle and both of us (me and bike) were very happy when it sold out.

This new edition has been completely revised and updated. And it continues to be an independent, DIY project. We've sold a few ads to help us cover the costs of printing and paper, but nobody pays to be included in *Get Lost!*

While we were unable to get any hemp paper for this edition, we're happy to be using vegetable-based inks. The book is printed on 100% post-consumer-waste recycled paper. It also now has a stitched binding.

I've tried to be very accurate with regard to prices, opening times, etc, but I'm just a goof, and things change (all the time). I love getting mail, so feel free to write if you have any suggestions, complaints, or spare change.

Be sure to check the Get Lost Publishing website on the internet for updates on the places and info included in *The Cool Guide*.

Thanks for buying this edition of *Get Lost!* Have a great trip!

Get Lost!
Box 18521
1001 WB Amsterdam
The Netherlands

Home Page:
http://www.xs4all.nl/~getlost

Also Available:
Get Lost! The Cool Guide to San Francisco
Get Lost! Der Coole Reiseführer - Amsterdam

CONTENTS

ABOUT THE AUTHOR

Joe Pauker was born at the summit of Mount Everest. Minutes after his birth, a blizzard froze almost everyone on the expedition. The only survivors were one Sherpa and the baby. Surprisingly, the infant thrived during the journey down the mountain, and was later passed from family to family until he ended up in South East Asia making shoes for a multinational company. By the time he was 10 he'd had enough and escaped from the Nike compound to begin his many years of travelling. During this period he played Godzilla in a Japanese film, fought against Franco in the Spanish Civil War, and coined the term "dot com". Joe was married briefly, but divorced after appearing as a guest on the Jerry Springer show, where he discovered that his wife was really a mormon. The experience wounded him deeply, but he found solace in song and soon became a member of a well-known boy band. After a year of constant touring, exhaustion began to threaten his complexion, so he quit the Backstreet Boys and fled to Amsterdam to pursue a career in writing. He is the author of one guide, an epic poem, and two plays. Joe Pauker died in 2001 after contracting the Ebola virus at an airport in Canada. He was only 19.

PLACES TO SLEEP

Accommodation is probably going to be the most expensive part of your stay in Amsterdam. Although there's an abundance of luxury hotel rooms, there just aren't enough inexpensive ones for all the budget-minded visitors to the city. It can be a real drag finding a place to stay - especially during the summer - and if you're in town for just a few days you don't want to waste time, so here are a few hints to help you out.

One possibility is to go with a "runner" (someone who has the shitty job of running back and forth between a hotel and the train station). These people work for small hotels or hostels, or for private homes and guest houses. A lot of the runners carry books with photos of the rooms so you can look at what you're going to be offered before trekking over there. The hotels tend to be dives, but I've found a couple of great private places this way. Go with your instincts: if you don't like the person offering you a room, tell them to forget it.

In the summer, a bed in a hostel runs anywhere from about ƒ25 to ƒ40 and a clean double room for less than ƒ140 is a good deal. In winter (except around holidays) it never hurts to bargain, and on weekdays double rooms can be found for as little as ƒ80.

At the Amsterdam Tourist Office (a.k.a. the VVV; across the square in front of Central Station and to your left, or in the station on Platform 2) they have a room-finding service. They can book you a dorm bed at a cheaper price, but plain double rooms in high season start at ƒ100 (without bath) and of course these go fast. If you use this service you'll have to pay them a ƒ5 per person service charge, and another ƒ5 per person as a deposit (which is later deducted from the price of the room). The people who work at the VVV are very nice and sometimes you can get a good deal, but in high season the line-ups are painfully long and slow.

The GWK bank (627-2731) at Central Station also offers a room-finding service. There you pay a ƒ10 per person fee (up to a maximum of ƒ20) and the full amount of the hotel in advance. The fact that you can't see the place first is a drawback, but their "same-day" sell-off rates (on all grades of hotels) are sometimes a real bargain, especially off-season.

To secure a room before leaving home, try The Netherlands Reservation Service (tel: 3170-419-5519 / fax: 3170-419-5544). This *free* service processes bookings for all grades of hotels throughout Holland. Just let them know what you want, when, and how much you're willing to pay. It's best to do this with a credit card number. If you don't have one you can still make a reservation, but you'll have to check in early in the day. Open: mon-fri 9-17.`

HOSTELS

Schiphol Airport

You know, I've slept in a lot of airports around the world, and Schiphol is definitely the best. They have comfortable couches in the *departure* lounges (that's in the boarding area, not in the rest of the airport) where you can actually lie down when you crash out. This area is only accessible to passengers until midnight. Before you check in, hit the Food Village supermarket (open daily 6-24:00) on the arrivals level.

It's the cheapest place in the airport for food. If you need to bathe there are *free* showers next to the British Airways lounge. (Like the good couches, they're in the boarding area.) Or else go to the Hotel Mercure (604-1339) near gate "F". They offer showers 24 hours a day in a private cabin (including soap, towel, and a hair dryer) for ƒ25, or a sauna and shower for ƒ30. As for breakfast, there are often free cheese samples on offer at the duty-free delicatessen. And upstairs, in the Panorama Lounge, they sell a few reasonably-priced snacks. Of course, you wouldn't want to stay there for your whole trip, but if you have a morning flight it's a good way to save the cost of a night's lodging.

Christian Youth Hostels (The Shelter City, The Shelter Jordan)
http://www.shelter.nl

Only ƒ20 to ƒ30 for a dorm bed and breakfast makes these two hostels a great deal. But separate rooms for men and women, curfews, sing-alongs in the lounge, and a clean-cut staff that's looking for converts should be enough to persuade you to spend a little more elsewhere. You'll have to find the addresses yourself.

The Flying Pig - *Nieuwendijk 100, 420-6822; Vossiusstraat 46-47, 400-4187*
http://www.flyingpig.nl

The guys who run these places are travellers themselves, which explains such things as the free use of kitchens, late night bars, free internet access, and the absence of curfews. For hanging out, both locations have lounges, and Nieuwendijk has DJs. All rooms have toilets and showers. Prices include a free, basic breakfast. The hostel on Nieuwendijk (Flying Pig Downtown), is very close to Central Station. The rates per person for shared rooms with 4 to 30 beds range, depending on the season, from ƒ34.50 to ƒ49.50. They also have a girls-only dorm. The other hostel (Flying Pig Palace) is by Vondelpark. They have shared rooms with 4 to 12 beds for ƒ34.50 to ƒ48.50 per person. A ƒ35 deposit for sheets and keys is returned when you leave. Both sites are central, but the neighbourhood around Vondelpark is much nicer. To reach the Palace from Central Station take tram 1, 2, or 5 to Leidseplein. Walk over the bridge to Vondelpark. The street runs along the left side of the park. (Map areas D4, B8)

Bob's Youth Palace - *Nieuwezijds Voorburgwal 92, 623-0063*

You can usually find this hostel by looking for a bunch of people sitting on the front steps smoking joints and strumming guitars. This is a pretty cool, clean place where a lot of travellers stay. It's right in the centre of the city and ƒ30 gets you a dorm bed and breakfast. They also have a women's dorm. Trams 1, 2, 5, 13 or 17 will take you there, or you can walk from Central Station: it's not far. (Map D4)

International Youth Hostels - *Zandpad 5 (Vondelpark), 589-8996; Kloveniersburgwal 97, 624-6832*
http://www.njhc.org/vondelpark

These are "official" youth hostels. The one in Vondelpark (a great location) has been completely renovated and all their rooms are equipped with a toilet and shower. They offer dorm beds (ƒ39.50 to ƒ48), double rooms (ƒ112.50 to ƒ150 per room), and quad rooms (ƒ185 to ƒ213 per room). Members pay ƒ5 less. Sheets are included in the price, as is an all-you-can-eat breakfast. There are also restaurants, a bicycle rental service, internet facilities, and a tourist info centre. And I've been assured that, most of the time, groups of kids on field trips will be booked into a different build-

ing from the one housing independent travellers. From Central Station take tram 1, 2 or 5 to Leidseplein. Walk to the Marriott Hotel and turn left. The hostel sign is just a block ahead of you. The other location is also nice: on a wide canal right in the centre of the city. There are only dorm rooms there, however. Beds cost from ƒ37.50 to ƒ42 (ƒ5 less if you're a member). (Map areas E6, B7)

The Bulldog - *Oudezijds Voorburgwal 220, 620-3822*
http://www.bulldog.nl/hotel

This hostel is located right in the Red Light District. The cheapest dorm beds go for ƒ35.50 to ƒ42, depending on the season. Smaller dorms with 8 beds and a shower and toilet in the room, run from ƒ42 to ƒ49.50 per person. Some of the dorms even have TVs. A coin that gets you 8 minutes worth of hot water in the shower is included in these prices. Extra coins cost ƒ1. If you need them, sheets are ƒ7.50. The rooms are very basic, but clean, there's no curfew or lock-out, and breakfast is included. There's also a DVD lounge, a chill lounge and a computer lounge. Single rooms go for ƒ109 to ƒ128; doubles for ƒ123 to ƒ136 (with shower and toilet - ƒ150 to ƒ160); triples and quads for ƒ59.50 to ƒ66 per person. They're also building a roof-top terrace, which will be great in the summer. (Map area D5)

HOTELS

Hemp Hotel Amsterdam - *Frederiksplein 15, 625-4425*
http://www.hemp-hotel.com

This little pension in the centre of Amsterdam is totally unique. The five small rooms, all decked out in hemp, each have their own theme. Try sleeping on a hemp mattress for a few nights in the Afghani room. Or, if you've always fancied a visit to the Himalayas, book the Indian room. Rates that include a vegetarian breakfast are ƒ100 for a single, ƒ140 for a double, ƒ145 for a twin with private shower. An extra mattress in the room costs an additional ƒ20. Look for a drop of about 10% off-season. Downstairs, the Hemple Temple bar has turned into a popular late-night hangout. You can party there until 3 on weeknights and 4 on Friday and Saturday. They serve hemp snacks, hemp beer, and delicious hemp vodka right out of the freezer! Take tram 4 from Central Station to Frederiksplein. (Map area E8)

Hotel Princess - *Overtoom 80, 612-2947*

This hotel is located at the corner of a busy intersection about a five-minute walk from Leidseplein. It's a budget hotel with some nice touches like reading lights by the bed, and mirrors. Single rooms are ƒ60 to ƒ80. Doubles start at ƒ100 and go up to ƒ140 for rooms with a private shower and toilet. Triples are ƒ135 to ƒ160. Quads: ƒ160 to ƒ200. You can request a double bed. Breakfast is included and it's simple, but excellent: bread, cheese, ham, cereal, boiled eggs, juice and coffee. The rest of the day, drinks and snacks are available at the reception. Take tram 1 from Central Station to Constantijn Huygensstraat. (Map area B7)

Hotel Crystal - *2e Helmersstraat 6, 618-0521*

Brought to you by the same owners as the Princess, Hotel Crystal is also close to Leidseplein, but on a quieter street. Singles go for ƒ70 to ƒ90, doubles without facilities for ƒ120 to ƒ140. Doubles with shower, toilet, and TV go for ƒ150 to ƒ200. Triples and quads are available, and all rooms will have TVs soon. An all-you-can-

eat breakfast is included here, too. From Central Station take tram 1 to Overtoom and then walk two blocks along Nassaukade. (Map area B6)

Hotel Abba - *Overtoom 122, 618-3058*

This is another hotel with friendly, helpful staff. An all-you-can-eat breakfast in a sunny room is included in the price. Depending on the season, singles cost from ƒ60 to ƒ75. Doubles (some with shower and toilet) range from ƒ90 to ƒ150. They also have rooms for 3 to 5 people that run ƒ50 to ƒ65 per person. There's a nice view from the front (especially from the upper floors), but it can be a bit noisy because of the street. Most of the rooms have been refurbished, with phones and TVs added. The free safety-deposit boxes in the reception area are a very nice feature: use them! Close to Leidseplein and Vondelpark. Tram 1 from Central Station to Constantijn Huygensstraat. (Map area A7)

Get Lucky Guest House - *Keizersgracht 705, 420-6466*
http://www.getluckyamsterdam.com

While it's definitely not your average hotel (let's just say it's a little unconventional), the four cosy guest rooms in this old canal house have all been renovated, and at ƒ80 to ƒ175 per night for a double, they're a pretty good deal. The location is great - close to everything - and most of the rooms have a beautiful canal view. The owners are more than happy to give you tourist info, or you can hang out in the comfy lounge and pick up some tips from other travellers. Oh yeah, and there's a PC in every room. It's a good idea to call and book in advance because this is a popular little place. Take tram 4 from Central Station to Keizersgracht. It's right there. (Map area E7)

The Flying Pig - *Nieuwendijk 100, 420-68; Vossiusstraat 46-47, 400-4187*

Both these hostels have twin rooms with shower and toilet for ƒ125 to ƒ150. See the Hostels section (above) for more details.

Groenendael - *Nieuwendijk 15, 624-4822*

If you prefer to stay close to the centre of town, then this hotel is a good deal. Singles go for ƒ65, doubles for ƒ100, and triples for ƒ150 (cheaper off season). Showers and toilets are in the hall. Breakfast is included. The rooms are tiny and pretty basic, but you're paying for the location. There's a lounge where you can hang out and meet people. The street is a little sleazy, but it's not dangerous. From Central Station, walk or run. (Map area D3)

Arena - *'s Gravesandestraat 51, 694-7444*
http://www.hotelarena.nl

Years ago, this huge, old mansion was converted into a low-budget hostel because the City wanted hippies to stop sleeping in Vondelpark. It turned into one of the coolest hostels in town, in spite of being located a bit outside of the centre. Now the dorms are gone and they only rent rooms. Depending on the season, doubles go for ƒ150 to ƒ275, triples for ƒ190 to ƒ240, and quads for ƒ250 to ƒ300. No breakfast is included. However, all rooms have shower and toilet, TV, telephone, and the very important reading lights by the bed. As always, it's a good idea to make a reservation. Close to the Tropenmuseum. From Central Station take tram 9 to Mauritskade. Night bus 76 or 77. (Map area G8)

Hotel Aspen - *Raadhuisstraat 31, 626-6714*

Singles here start at ƒ65. A nice-sized, double room with shower and toilet costs ƒ135. Doubles with sink only start at ƒ80. Triples and quads go for ƒ180, both with shower and toilet. No breakfast, but a great location close to Dam Square and Anne Frank House. There are a bunch of hotels here in the beautiful Art Nouveau "Utrecht Building". From Central Station take tram 13 or 17 to Westermarkt and walk back half a block. If you don't have much luggage, it's only a 10 or 15 minute walk. (Map area C4)

Van Ostade Bicycle Hotel - *Van Ostadestraat 123, 679-3452*

If you're travelling by bicycle take note. This is one of the only hotels in Amsterdam with free indoor bike parking. They also rent bikes to guests for ƒ10 per day and provide info on tours in and out of Amsterdam. The rooms? ƒ130 for a single. ƒ125 to ƒ185 for doubles. Breakfast is included. The rooms aren't exciting, but they're clean and all now have TVs. There's a library/lounge downstairs. It's close to the Albert Cuyp market. Follow tram 24 or 25 from Central Station to Ceintuurbaan and then go one block further.

Black Tulip Hotel - *Gelderskade 16, 427-0933*
http://www.blacktulip.nl

I should start by saying that this hotel, situated in a 16th century canal house near Central Station, caters exclusively to leather men. That is, gay men who are seriously into S/M, B&D and leather fetish. Each of the nine luxurious rooms is decorated differently, but all feature kinky sex equipment: metal cages, stocks, fist-fuck chairs, etc. In addition to a sling and bondage hooks, all rooms have TVs with VCRs, minibars, telephones, and private bathrooms (some with whirlpool). Prices range from ƒ220 to ƒ370 and include a buffet breakfast in their comfortable lounge. And, as a service to guests who prefer to travel light, they rent big, heavy, leather boots and other paraphernalia here, too. (Map area E4)

A bed at the Black Tulip.

Hotel Rembrandt - *Plantage Middenlaan 17, 627-2714*

This is a sweet little hotel in a beautiful, wealthy area of town. All rooms have a TV and a coffee/tea maker, but if you've got the dough, splurge on the more expensive doubles (ƒ180 to ƒ200 per room). Each of those rooms is uniquely decorated, has a modern bathroom, and is way nicer than what you normally get for that price in Amsterdam. Other doubles cost ƒ130 to ƒ140 per night, with shower and toilet in the hall. Sometimes they can squeeze in an extra person for ƒ40. Quad rooms cost ƒ280 to ƒ300. Breakfast is included in an incredible, antique-filled room. The Botanical Gardens (see Museums chapter) is two minutes away, and just beyond that, the Waterlooplein market. From Central Station take tram 9 to Plantage Kerklaan and then walk back half a block.

Amstel Botel - *Oosterdokskade 2-4, 626-4247*

It's not really cheap to stay at this 4-story, floating hotel, but if you've got a little extra money it's sort of unique to stay on a boat. The rooms are small, but very clean and modern. They all have a tiny shower and toilet, a phone, and a TV with free in-house videos and a movie channel. The reception is open 24 hours and they don't charge commission to change money. Rooms with a double bed or two single beds cost ƒ147 to ƒ164; singles cost ƒ129 to ƒ139. There are also some triple rooms for ƒ195. Prices drop ƒ10 in the winter. Breakfast is not included. Make sure you get a room over-looking the water. Located just a couple of minutes walk east of Central Station, a walk that can be a bit creepy at night. (Map area F3)

Amsterdam Houseboat Rentals - *427-3807*
http://www.amsterdamhouseboats.com

This new company rents beautiful, luxuriously-furnished houseboats. They all have big-screen TVs, CD players, broadband internet connections, complete kitchens, and outdoor chill spaces. There's also a cell-phone with ƒ25 prepaid. The 1000 US dol-lar a week price tag sounds expensive, but the boats sleep 4 (one of them 5) so if you break it down it's not much more than a budget hotel, only you'll be stylin'. Book early: they go fast.

Xaviera Hollander's Bed and Breakfast - *Stadionweg 17, 673-3934*
http://www.xs4all.nl/~xaviera

I know that 125 US dollars a night isn't cheap, but this is the home of a real celebri-ty. Xaviera Hollander's house is in the wealthy area of Amsterdam South. She rents two rooms to visitors. Both have TVs and king-size beds, and of course, breakfast is included. Prices sometimes drop off-season or for long stays. Go to the website to see pictures of the rooms, and to read about all the creative projects Xaviera's got going. The Happy Hooker has a guest house: that *had* to be in The Cool Guide.

CAMPING

Zeeburg - *Zuider IJdijk 20, 694-4430*

They have all kinds of facilities here, including a funky bar that throws regular par-ties in the summer. Camping costs ƒ8 per person plus ƒ6.50 per tent. There are also "camping huts" with beds at ƒ32.50 per person. Open all year. Take the metro to Amstel Station, then bus 37, and then it's a 2 minute walk. Night bus 77 or 79 (20 minute walk).

Gaasper Camping - *Loosdrechtdreef 7, 696-7326*

ƒ8 per adult, ƒ3.50 per kid, ƒ4.50 per dog (plus ƒ8.75 for a 2-person tent, ƒ10.75 for a 3-or-more-person tent, and ƒ7.50 per car). Open March 15th to December 31st. Take the metro from Central Station to Gaasperplein.

Amsterdamse Bos - *Kleine Noorddijk 1, 641-6868*

There's a campsite here in the beautiful woods just south of the city centre. ƒ8.75 per person, ƒ5.50 per tent, ƒ4.75 per car. Open April 1st to October 31st. Bus 171 from Central Station. Ask the driver for the closest stop.

Vliegenbos - *Meeuwenlaan 138, 636-8855*

ƒ14.25 per person. And you'll be charged extra if you have a vehicle. There are also 30 cabins (four beds each) that rent for ƒ80 a night. They accept written reservations for the cabins from March. Open April 1st to September 30th. Buses 32, 36. Night bus 73.

GETTING AROUND

Central Amsterdam's old cobblestone streets are great for wandering through and getting lost. And fortunately, Amsterdam is full of people who speak English (to get you found). But, actually, you shouldn't have too much trouble if you take a few minutes to study a map. Detailed maps are available all over. Buy one: they're only about ƒ5 and the street names listed on the back will make it easy to quickly find the places mentioned in this book.

If you really can't afford to buy a map, there are also a variety of free ones available around town: the Amsterdam Diamond Center (Rokin 1-5) offers maps of the city centre; both High View and the BCD (Cannabis Retailers' Association) produce advertising maps that are available in many coffeeshops; the Gay Tourist Map is free at Pink Point (see Practical Shit); and at tourist locations you'll find a *Visitors Guide* published by the Yellow Pages that includes a pretty good map. Finally, you can always use the one found in the front pages of the telephone book - it's fairly detailed and includes a street registry.

Online, go to *http://www.amsterdam.nl/kaart/e_map.html*. Type in the address of your hotel or any other place in Amsterdam and it loads a printable map of the street, neighbourhood, or whole city with your destination clearly marked.

The basic layout of the city, with a series of horseshoe-shaped canals surrounding the oldest part, makes it fairly easy to find your way on foot. This is certainly the best way to see Amsterdam and fully appreciate its incredible beauty.

BICYCLES

Don't be scared to rent a bike and go for an authentic Amsterdam experience. Unlike most North American and many European cities, bikes are respected in Amsterdam. There are still too many dirty, ugly, polluting cars in the city centre, but there are also thousands of beautiful, clean, fast, efficient bicycles. There are bike lanes all over the city and it's a fun, relatively safe way to explore. Listed below are several places to rent bikes. If you're here for awhile you may want to consider

Buttman at a bike demo.

buying a used bike and selling it to someone when you leave. Make sure you lock your bike everywhere, even if you're only leaving it for an instant (see note on bike theft). One of the cheapest places to buy a lock is the Waterlooplein flea market (see Markets, Shopping chapter).

I've never been on an organized bike tour in Amsterdam, but if you're more comfortable riding with a group, Mike's Bike Tours (622-7970; *http://www.mikesbiketours.com*) does both inner-city and countryside trips from the beginning of April until the end of October. Another option is to contact the tour organizers at the funky new student-run organization, AmsterdamBackDoor. Let them know what you're into and they'll design a tour to suit your needs and interests. Their excellent website (*http://www.amsterdambackdoor.com*) is updated weekly.

A fun day to get on a bike is the annual Autovrije Zondag (Auto-free Sunday; *http://www.autovrijezondag.nl*). It takes place in mid to late September, and even though the cab drivers are still allowed to drive like idiots through the city, a good portion of the centre is closed to motorized traffic.

Macbike - *Mr. Visserplein 2, 620-0985; Marnixstraat 220, 626 6964; Weteringschans 2 (opening Sept. 2001)*
http://www.macbike.nl

Good quality bikes and a good reputation. They also have maps and information on cycling routes in and outside the city. ƒ12.50 per day plus ƒ50 and passport, or else a credit card. Special weekly rate: ƒ60. Theft insurance (optional) costs an extra 50%. Open: daily 9-18. (Map areas B5, E6, C7)

Bike City - *Bloemgracht 70, 626-3721*
http://www.bikecity.nl

This is a genuinely friendly shop located on a beautiful canal near the Anne Frank House. Standard bikes cost ƒ12.50 per day (ƒ10 for each extra day) and the weekly rate is ƒ50. They also rent 3-speed bikes with hand-brakes (ƒ17.50 per day) and 5 speed mountain bikes (ƒ22.50 per day). If you ask, you'll also be provided with a puncture repair kit - a bonus if you're heading for the countryside. A cash deposit of ƒ50 and a passport are required. Open: daily 9-18. Closed in winter. (Map area B4)

Rent-A-Bike-Damstraat - *Pieterjacobszdwarsstraat 11, 625-5029*
http://www.bikes.nl

You'll find Rent-A-Bike in an alley off Damstraat just east of Dam Square. They're also very friendly. Keep your eyes peeled for their small coupons that get you a 10% discount. The only drawback to renting here is the big sign on the front of their bikes that scream "tourist". ƒ15 per day, but the more days you rent the cheaper it gets. Their special weekly rate is ƒ76.50. ƒ50 deposit plus a passport, or else a credit card. Seats and helmets for kids are also available. Open: daily 9-18. (Map area D5)

Frédéric Rent a Bike - *Brouwersgracht 78, 624-5509*

It's just a 10-minute walk from Central Station to this small shop. They only charge ƒ10 a day, ƒ50 a week. Open daily 9-18. (Map area D3)

Take-A-Bike - *Stationplein, 624-8391*

Out the main doors at Central Station and to your left. It's cheap, but kinda sleazy down here. ƒ11,25 per day. ƒ200 deposit. Special weekly rate: ƒ45. Open: daily 8-22. (Map area E3)

A NOTE ON BIKE THIEF MOTHERFUCKERS

Last year in Amsterdam over 150,000 bikes were stolen. Hot bikes are sold by sorry looking junkies who cruise around mumbling "fiets te koop", but more bikes are actually stolen by organised gangs. Junkies sell hot bikes very cheaply, but if you're tempted to buy one while you're here, think again. When you buy a stolen bike you're hurting the person who owned it, as well as keeping the asshole who nicked it in business. And I don't want to lose my transportation just because you want a cheap bike.

De Rommelmarkt - *Looiersgracht 38*

If you're interested in buying a used bike, check the big tree by the entrance to this flea market (see Markets, Shopping chapter): sometimes there are a few leaning against it. If you're lucky, you might find something for ƒ50 to ƒ100. Wednesday and Saturday are the best days to look. Open: 11-17. (Map area B6)

Binnenpret - *1e Schinkelstraat 14, tel: 0651-720911*

Another place to buy a cheap bike is at the shop in a shed in the courtyard of this old squat. The guy who runs it sells very basic, refurbished bikes for ƒ80. He may have one on hand, but often you have to place an order and then pick it up later. Usually open: mon-fri 12-19.

Via Via - *626-6166*
http://www.viavia.nl

Via Via is a classified ads paper that's published every Tuesday and Thursday. It features thousands of articles for sale and is available all over town. Look under *Fietsen* or *Tweewielers*. There are always lots of cheap bikes listed, though you'll have to find a Dutch speaker to help you read the ads. The paper costs ƒ4.50, but you can peruse it at the library for free (see Hanging Out chapter).

Bike Wars - *Vondel Park; every couple of months (check the Get Lost website)*

Bike demolition derby time. Every couple of months a bunch of people meet at night at the open air theatre in Vondelpark (see Parks, Hanging Out Chapter), and with some heavy tunes playing in the background they ride around and smash the crap out of each others bikes until only one is left riding. Cool.

INLINE SKATES

Rodolfo's - *Sarphatistraat 59, 622-5488*
http://www.rodolfos.com

Inline skates for rent! Skating is not bad on the bike lanes and the people who work here at Europe's oldest skateshop know all the hot spots around town. The rental is from 12 noon to 11:00 the next day, and the price is ƒ15. A ƒ100 deposit and ID, or a credit card, is required. They also sell snowboards, skateboards, and skate fashions. Open: mon 13-18; tues-fri 10-18 (thurs 'til 21); sat 10-17. (Map area E8)

Rent A Skate - *tel: 06-54-66-2262*

Vondelpark is the best place to skate, especially if you're inexperienced and want to avoid auto traffic. Skates are rented by the café at the Amstelveenseweg end of Vondelpark, and by the café near the tennis courts in the middle of the park. You'll need ƒ10/hour plus a passport and ƒ50, or else a ƒ200 deposit. They're open (when the streets are dry) from May to October, daily, 11 to sunset; and on weekends from mid-March to May.

Friday Night Skate - *Vondelpark*
http://www.fridaynightskate.nl

As long as the roads are dry, skaters meet every Friday evening at 20:00 in front of the Film Museum in Vondelpark and head out for a tour through the city. Everyone is welcome, but you should be an experienced skater. (Map area B8)

SCOOTERS

Scooter Rental Service Amsterdam - *Marnixstraat 208-210, 420-1900*

Are you, like, born to be wild? But also kind and gentle? Then this place is for you. The rental includes insurance and a full tank of gas. One hour -ƒ15; second hour -ƒ12.50; third hour -ƒ10. Half day -ƒ50; full day -ƒ90. Bring your passport and credit card (for the ƒ1000 deposit). Open: daily 9-20 (summer); shorter hours in winter. (Map area B5)

PUBLIC TRANSPORT

Most people visiting Amsterdam stay mainly in the centre and don't have to rely too much on public transit. But if you need it, you'll find there's a good network of trams, buses and metro lines. The transit system operates largely on the honour system, so you can try to ride for free if you want, but if you get caught the "I'm a tourist; I didn't understand" routine usually won't work. The fine is ƒ60 plus the fare. And by law you have to show them some ID. The same year that South Africa did away with its oppressive pass laws, Holland introduced one. Figure that out while the transit police take you away. It happens!

Amsterdam is divided into zones, and the more zones you travel in the more expensive your ticket will be. If you'll be using public transit for more than one round trip your best bet is to buy a 15 strip *strippenkaart* for ƒ12.50. Most of central Amsterdam is one zone. For each ride in the centre you must stamp two strips on your card. You can do it yourself in one of the yellow boxes you'll find in most trams and metro stations, or you can ask the driver or tram conductor to do it for you. Your ticket is then valid for an hour within that zone (the last in the series of numbers stamped on your ticket is the time you embarked). You have to stamp an extra strip for each additional zone you want to travel in or through - one zone costs two strips, two zones cost three strips, etc. Buy these *strippenkaarten* at Central Station, post offices, tobacco shops or some supermarkets. Single tickets can be purchased on trams and buses, but they're much more expensive (ƒ3). You can also purchase day tickets that are good on all buses, trams, and the metro (subway) from 1- 9 days (1 day -ƒ12.50; 2 days -ƒ17.50; 3 days -ƒ22; 4 days -ƒ27). After midnight, night buses take over, but only on some routes, and the prices go up. To disembark your train, tram or bus, push the button by the door.

The "circle-tram 20" runs in a loop around Amsterdam, starting at Central Station and stopping at most of the major tourist sites. The day tickets mentioned above can be bought from the conductor on this line.

There's a great new mini-bus service called the Opstapper that runs from Central Station, along the Brouwersgracht, Prinsengracht, Amstel, and ends at the Stopera (see Free Concerts, Hanging Out Chapter). There are no stops: you can flag it down and get on or off anywhere along the route. It's a one zone fare and you can use your *strippenkaart*.

For more information and a shitty, free route map (or a better one for ƒ1.50) stop by the GVB (public transit) ticket office. Walk across the little square in front of Central Station and you'll find it on your left, next to the Tourist Office. You can also call 0900-9292 for directions, but it costs 75 cents per minute and I've found that they often give bad advice. Perhaps it's a feeble attempt to get the public to support the privatization of public transit, which will take place sometime in 2002. When that happens, expect prices to go up and service to go downhill. GVB open: mon-fri 7-21; sat/sun 8-21.

CARS

Parking

There are already too many fucking cars in Amsterdam, but if you have to bring one into the city the best thing to do is put it in a garage and leave it there. It's expensive, but nowhere near as much as if you get caught parking illegally. The most reasonably priced is the Arena/Transferium (tel: 400-1721), a huge garage under a stadium south of the city centre (from the A10 take exit A9/A2 and exit at Ouderkerk aan de Amstel). Parking there costs ƒ3 an hour, ƒ12.50 a day, or ƒ30 for 24 hours. Ask at the counter and they'll give you two free metro (subway) tickets to the centre and back. Innercity parking is much more expensive. At Europarking (Marnixstraat 250, 623-6694), the price is ƒ4.50 an hour, up to a maximum of ƒ60 a day. They're open: mon-thurs 6:30-1:00; fri/sat 6:30-2:00; sun 7-1:00. (Map area B5). ANVB Parking (Prins Hendrikkade 20a) costs ƒ4.50/hour or ƒ45/day and it's open 24 hours. (Map area D3)

Parking on the street costs an average of ƒ5 an hour, depending on the neighbourhood you're in and the time of day. You pay at little blue boxes that are on every block, and the instructions are in English. There are still a few area outside of the centre with free street parking (Buikslotermeerplein, Diemen Zuid, Gaasperplas), but by the time you read this, that may be history.

Warning: wheel clamping of illegally parked cars is very common in Amsterdam. If it happens, you'll have go to an inconveniently located office to pay your ticket (about ƒ140) and then wait for someone to come around and unclamp your car. If you leave it, your car will be towed. Then you can expect to pay over ƒ400 to get it back!

Car Rental

If you want to rent a car, look in the yellow pages under *Autoverhuur*. The cheapest I've found is Kuperus, in the east end (Van der Madeweg 1, 668-3311), but the guys who work there are exceedingly unpleasant. It might be worth it to pay a bit more somewhere else. If you don't mind hopping the train out to Zaandam (a 20 minute, less than ƒ5 ride from Amsterdam) you can style in a Mercedes from easyRentacar (*http://www.easyrentacar.com*) for ƒ35 a day. Note that if you can provide an Amsterdam address for the rental agreement, you might get a better deal from the major rental companies as some have special rates for residents.

24 Hour Gas Stations

There are gas stations open 24 hours at Sarphatistraat 225 and Marnixstraat 250. Please remember when you're buying gas, that Shell Oil helped prop up the apartheid regime in South Africa. They also supported the corrupt military dictatorship in Nigeria that murdered Ken Saro-Wiwa and so many other Ogoni people. Shell isn't the only sleazy oil company around, but they are the target of a world-wide boycott. Hit the greedy bastards where it hurts them the most: in their pockets.

Taxis

They're expensive, and they treat cyclists like shit, but if you really need one call 677-7777 and enjoy the service: taxis here are very comfortable. You can't flag one down on the street, but there are taxi stands at Central Station, Dam Square, Leidseplein, Rembrandtplein, Nieuwmarkt, Haarlemmerpoort, the Tropenmuseum, etc.

BOATS

Tours

Boat tours leave from several docks in front of Central Station and along the Damrak. It's very touristy, but I think it's fun to see the city from the canal perspective, and some of the taped info is interesting. The tours usually give you a quick look at the harbour and then cruise along the canals while a recording in four languages describes the sights. The routes vary slightly, last one hour, depart every twenty minutes or so, and cost about *f*13. The canals are particularly beautiful at night. The last tours depart at 22:00 and are often sold out in advance.

Motor Boats

Ahoy matey! In the summer, Sesa Rent A Boat (509-5050, *http://www.sesa.nl*) has motor boats that seat up to 10 people. And they're electric, which means you won't be polluting the canals with oil and noise. The cost is *f*80 per hour (*f*100 per hour in summer) and you must provide identification and a *f*300 deposit. Located at Kloveniersburgwal 23, by the Nieuwmarkt. Open 10-22. (Map area D5)

Canal Motorboats (422-7007) is another company that rents electric motorboats. These seat 6 and rent for *f*65 for 1 hour; *f*110 for 2 hours; *f*150 for 3 hours; and *f*25 for every hour after that. You'll need ID and a *f*300 deposit. Bring some food and sit back: they don't go very fast. Located at Oosterdoksade 5 (just east of Central Station). Both these rental companies are open - weather permitting - from spring to fall, 10-22:00. (Map area F4)

Ferries

Behind Central Station, you'll find free ferries that make the brief journey to North Amsterdam every few minutes. You can take your bike on with you and it's a good starting point if you want to ride out into the countryside. Most of the bike rental places will give you free info about scenic routes.

Canal Bikes

Canal bikes, 2-4 person pedal bikes, are all over the old city canals in summer and look like a lot of fun. They can be rented at several locations including in front of the Rijksmuseum, near Leidseplein, and Anne Frank House. One or two people pay *f*12.50/hour each; 3 or more people pay *f*10/hour each. Deposit *f*50. Tel: 626-5574 (*http://www.canalbike.nl*). Open: in summer 10-18 ('til 21:30 if the weather is really nice); and in winter, at the Rijksmuseum dock, 10-17:30.

GETTING OUT OF AMSTERDAM

TRAIN

Travelling by train is certainly the most pleasant and comfortable way to get around Europe, but it can also be very expensive. On some routes you have to reserve a seat (and pay a reservation fee) even if the train isn't full, which seems kind of ludicrous; but in the summertime it's a good idea to book a seat even if it isn't mandatory. The booking office for international train journeys is just to the left as you enter the main hall of Central Station. Grab a number and be prepared to wait. Tickets for destinations within Holland can be bought at the windows to the right of the main hall, or from the big yellow machines (which have instructions in English). For international train info and reservations by phone, call 0900-9296 (ƒ.50/min); for trains within the Netherlands, dial 0900 9292 (ƒ.75/min). Online, go to: http://www.ns.nl

Thalys - *0900-9296 (ƒ.50/min)*
http://www.thalys.com

Here's a tip. If you're planning to go from Amsterdam to Paris, you can ride this high-speed train from Central Station to Gare du Nord for only ƒ158 return. It's a little more expensive than the bus, but takes only about half the time (4 hours), and it's *much* more comfortable. There are only a few seats offered at this price on each train, however, so book early.

BUS

Eurolines - *Rokin 10; Amstel Station, 560-8788*
http://www.eurolines.nl

Eurolines has service to almost 400 destinations. I've had both good and bad experiences with this company, but they are much cheaper than the train, especially off-season. Check it out early because not all routes are served daily and they often sell out in advance. Keep in mind that border checks, especially going into France, tend to be a *lot* more severe on buses than on other modes of transport. You must have your passport number to buy a ticket. Rokin office open: mon-fri 9:30-17:30 (thurs 'til 20); sat 11-17. Amstel Station office open: mon-fri 7-22:30. (Map area D5)

HITCHING

There is a lot of competition hitching out of Amsterdam in the summer, but people do give lifts. Hitching isn't allowed on the national highways. Stay on the on-ramps or in gas stations. You'll avoid hassles from the cops and, anyway, it's easier for drivers to pick you up. If you're heading to Utrecht, take tram 25 to the end of the line and join the crowd on the Utrechtseweg. How about southern or central Germany? Hop the metro to Amstel station and try your luck on the Gooiseweg. For Rotterdam and The Hague go by tram 4 to the RAI convention centre and walk down Europaboulevard until you see the entrance to the A2 highway. But before you hit the road, check http://www.hitchhikers.org and see if you can arrange a ride without breathing exhaust. Good luck.

AIR TRAVEL

Budget Travel Agencies

The NBBS is the official Dutch student travel agency and, despite the rude staff I've encountered at some of their shops, it's worth checking them out if you're looking for an air ticket. Don't bother calling them - it's an expensive pay number. They have offices at Haarlemmerstraat 115, and Rokin 66 (just south of Dam Square). Be prepared for a wait. There are several other budget travel agencies in the same area. Budget Air is at Rokin 34 (627-1251), and for last minute deals (mostly to southern Europe and North Africa) pop into L'tur at Rokin 40 (421-1583; *http:// www.ltur-ams.com*), or the Martinair counter at Schiphol Airport (601-1767). I had a good experience recently at D-reizen (Linnaeusstraat 112; 200-1012), which is part of a big chain. They've got good last minute deals with different airlines for two people travelling together. World Ticket Center (Nieuwezijds Voorburgwal 159, 626-1011) sometimes has good specials and the consultants there are very nice. Note that all travel agencies in Amsterdam tack on a ridiculous, rip-off "service charge" of about ƒ25. For a complete listing of travel agencies look in the phone book (the white pages) under *Reisbureau*. Shop around.

Call and Go - *tel: 023-567-4567*

This phone line (run by the Dutch airline, KLM) is updated daily with good deals on next-day departures to all sorts of destinations. The recorded message is in Dutch and English. If you stay on the line after the message ends, you'll be connected with KLM reservations. Unfortunately, there are only return tickets on offer and the maximum stay is 4 weeks. Open: daily 13-23.

Train to the Airport

Easy as pie! Hop on the train at Central Station (ƒ6.50) and you're at Schiphol Airport (*http://www.schiphol.nl*) in about 20 minutes. Trains depart regularly starting at about 4:45 in the morning 'til just after midnight. Then there's one train an hour starting at 00:42. Keep a close eye on your luggage! If you're travelling on KLM or Northwest, and your ticket was issued in the Netherlands you can use it to travel for free by train to and from Schiphol. (Did you know that Schiphol Airport is five metres below sea level?).

Bus to the Airport

The Interliner Bus rides between Leidseplein and the airport from about 5:30 to about midnight every day and costs ƒ5.50 one-way, and ƒ9.25 return. Call 0900-9292 (ƒ.75/min) for departure times. It's a bit cheaper than the train, but then you have to spend a guilder on the phone getting the information!

MAPS & TRAVEL BOOKS

à la Carte - *Utrechtsestraat 110-112, 625-0679*
Open: tues-fri 10-18 (in summer, thurs 'til 21); sat 10-17. (Map area E7)

Pied à Terre - *Singel 393, 627-4455*
http://www.piedaterre.nl
Open: mon-fri 11-18 (thurs 'til 21, apr 1- sept 1); sat 10-17. (Map area C5)

Boekhandel Jacob van Wijngaarden - *Overtoom 97, 612-1901*
http://www.jvw.nl
Open: mon 13-18; tues-fri 10-18 (thurs 'til 21); sat 10-17. (Map area A7)

Evenaar - *Singel 348, 624-6289*
(See Books & Magazines, Shopping chapter) Open: mon-fri 12-18; sat 11-17.

GETTING TO THE BEACH

Trains to Zandvoort (on the coast), leave from Central Station approximately every half hour. In the summer there are direct trains and on sunny days they're very crowded. Off-season you have to change trains in Haarlem. The trip takes about 30 minutes and costs ƒ8.50 one-way and ƒ15 return. You can bring your bike for an extra charge (ƒ12 return). Zandvoort can get very crowded, the water isn't exactly clean, and it's often very windy. But the beach is big, wide and white, and a day trip there can be a lot of fun. For the past few years, the hot party place to hang has been at Bloemendaal aan Zee, a 45 minute walk north along the beach from Zandvoort. Several pavillions there host regular parties. It's a bit of a meat market, but it can also be a relaxing place to kick back, listen to the music, and watch the sunset. Sometimes there's a beach-shuttle that'll take you there for about ƒ3, but usually you have to hoof it along the beach. Remember to check the departure time of the last train back to Amsterdam!

PRACTICAL SHIT

TOURIST INFO

The **Amsterdam Tourist Office** (a.k.a. the **VVV**) is Holland's official tourist agency. However, it's also a privately-run business, so even though the people working here are almost always patient and friendly, and can be very helpful, you can see that the word from on high is "sell, sell, sell". There's a branch inside Central Station, upstairs on platform 2 (open: mon-sat 8-20; sun 9-17), and another just to the left as you cross the square in front of the station (open: daily 9-17). There's also a branch at Leidseplein (open: mon-sat 9-19; sun 9-17). Be prepared for a long wait if you're here during high season. They have an info number, but it's very expensive (0900-400-4040; mon-fri 9-17; ƒ1 per minute). (Map area E3)

MONEY

The **Dutch currency** is the guilder and it's represented by any one of these abbreviations: NLG, Hfl, or ƒ. Coins come in annoying little 5 and 10 cent pieces (which you can get rid of in the candy machines in Central Station), 25 cents, 1, 2.50, and 5 guilders. Notes start at 10 guilders. Shops now also have to list prices in euros (€) in addition to guilders. The euro is the new single currency of the European Union. Nobody knows exactly what will happen when it goes into circulation in 2002, but you can be sure that it won't benefit you and me.

I hate fucking banks! They're all thieves and scum. That 1% surcharge you paid on your travellers cheques? Pure profit. They're already paid by the cheque companies to sell them! Then they've got the nerve to charge you commission when you cash them. However, **changing money** at bank alternatives in the tourist areas (like Leidseplein) is mostly a big rip-off, too: high commission charges and low rates. Beware of places that advertise "no commission" in big letters followed by fine print that says "if you're purchasing" (this means if you're giving them guiders to buy US $, for example). It's a scam, and once they have your money inside their bullet-proof glass booth you won't get it back. It's hard to recommend a place because they're changing all the time, but here are a few stable money-changers.

Pott-Change - *Damrak 95, 626-3658; Rembrandtplein 10, 626-8768*
> This place doesn't charge a commission to change non-Euro currencies, and only ƒ2.50 to cash non-Euro cheques. Open: mon-sat 8-20; sun 9-20. (Map area D4)

Lorentz Change - *Damrak 31, 420-6002*
> These guys by the Dam Hotel also offer good rates on cash and no commission on non-Euro currencies. Open: daily, 24 hours. (Map area D4)

Thomas Cook - *Damrak 1, 620-3236*
> They'll cash their own cheques free of charge, but they charge a *minimum* of ƒ10 to exchange cash, so watch out. Open: mon-sat 8-20; sun 9-20. (Map area E3)

GWK Bank - *Central Station, 627-2731*
> This member of the bank mafia charges 2.25% commission on the total amount

changed, plus ƒ5 - a rip-off - but they're conveniently located and open long hours. Open: daily 7-22:45 (Map area E3)

PHONE

To use a **phone booth** you'll need a phone card. They can be purchased in denominations of ƒ10 and ƒ25 at the Tourist Office, post offices, tobacco shops, and supermarkets. Phone booths have instructions in English. Pay phones that take coins are almost extinct.

For **long distance calls** dial 00, then your country code and the number. Holland's country code is 31. Amsterdam's city code is 20. Long-distance phone cards are available in most of the "call centres" on tourist strips like the Damrak, and at tobacco shops. They come in denominations of ƒ25 and ƒ50 and they can be a very good deal. Easy to use instructions, in English, are printed on the back of the cards.

LEFT LUGGAGE

The lockers at Central Station cost ƒ5.25 (small) and ƒ8.50 (large) for 24 hours. The maximum rental period is 72 hours at a time. They're accessible 'round the clock. If your stuff is too big for the lockers, there's a left luggage counter that charges ƒ12 per piece for 24 hours. It's a rip-off, but what can you do? The maximum storage time permitted here is 10 days. Left luggage open: daily 7-24. **Note**: like all big train stations, Central Station has its share of bag-snatchers hanging about. Never take your eyes off your luggage.

POST

The **main post office** is at Singel 250 (556-3311) at the corner of Raadhuisstraat, just west of Dam Square. Turn to your left inside the main entrance and take a number: no pushing, no shoving. The system here is very efficient and the people behind the counter speak English (like most Amsterdammers) and are genuinely friendly and helpful. Postcards take ƒ1 stamps. Letters up to 20 grams cost ƒ1.10 for Europe and ƒ1.60 overseas. In the same room are telephones, a photo-copier, a fax machine, and a passport photo booth. I like this place. The room to the right of the main entrance has a stationary store and a bank that changes money, but they're very slow and charge commission. The main post office is open: mon-fri 9-18 (thurs 'til 20); sat 10-13:30. (Map C4)

The entrance to the **Poste Restante** is down some stairs to the left of the entrance to the main post office. If you're having mail sent to you the address is: Poste Restante, Hoofdpostkantoor PTT, Singel 250, 1012 SJ, Amsterdam, The Netherlands. Don't forget to bring your passport when you go to pick up your letters.

There are also post offices at Haarlemmerdijk 99, Kerkstraat 167, Bloemgracht 300, Waterlooplein 2. But note that their opening hours are often shorter than those of the main office listed above. Before or after hours head to the sorting centre just east of Central Station (Oosterdokskade 3, 622-8272). They offer all postal services and a photocopier. They're open: mon-fri 7:30-21; sat 7:30-12. For more postal info call the **free customer service line**: 0800-0417 (choose "5" to speak to a human).

If you're posting letters from a **mailbox**, the right-hand slot is for Amsterdam, and the left side is for the rest of the world.

VOLTAGE

The electric current in Holland operates on 220 volts. If you're from Canada or the US, you'll have to get a converter and/or a transformer if you want to plug in anything that you've brought with you. Note that it's probably cheaper to by them in North America than in Holland.

WEATHER

Expect lousy weather. Then if it's warm and dry, you'll feel really lucky (which you will be). Bring layers of clothing and something waterproof. Umbrellas don't always do the trick, as this is a very windy country, especially in the fall. The North Sea wind also means that the weather can change very quickly and several times a day. Winters are cold, but it rarely goes below freezing. July and August are your best bet for nice weather (of course). Having said all that, Amsterdam is a fun city to visit any time of year.

PICKPOCKETS

Amsterdam is a very safe city and the only crime you're likely to witness or experience is pickpocketing. It's not a violent crime, but what a drag when it happens! Watch out for these assholes: they're very good at what they do. Keep your valuables safely stashed and watch your bags at all times. The worst areas are around Central Station, Dam Square, Leidseplein, and the Red Light District - in other words, tourist areas where you'll probably end up at least a couple of times during your stay. Try not to act like a total space cadet (in spite of how you might feel) and you probably won't have any problems. (If you do, see the Phone Numbers chapter for the services you'll need.)

DRUG TESTING

Hard drugs are illegal in Holland. Buying them from strangers can be dangerous. And anything you buy on the street is guaranteed to be crap. But if you've scored some ecstasy elsewhere, call the Stichting Adviesburo Drugs (623-7943). *They do not sell drugs here*. It's a non-profit foundation that, among other things, will test your ecstasy to see what it really is. A test costs only ƒ5. They take a sliver as a sample (you won't lose your hit), and within a couple of minutes they can tell you what you've bought. This is a fantastic service (anonymous too, by the way). By testing ecstasy they know what's on the market, and if something bad is going around they can help track it down and get it out of circulation. They test cocaine, too, but it takes a couple of days. Open: tues-fri 14-17.

GAY & LESBIAN INFO

The Cool Guide has never included a chapter geared specifically towards lesbian and gay visitors to Amsterdam. Instead, I've made a point of highlighting a couple of spots that cater to a mainly gay crowd in each section of the book (and any place that wasn't gay-friendly, wouldn't be listed). However, to find out more about what's happening on the gay scene around town, your first stop should be the fabulous Pink Point kiosk at Westermarkt (just across the street from the Homomonument). They provide all sorts of free info including the *Gay News*, and the bi-weekly fanzine *Shark*, which features an index of alternative queer venues and events. Pink Point also sells guidebooks and all kinds of unique queer souvenirs. Open: daily 12-18 (apr-sept 30). (Map area C4)

FOOD

Eating out in Amsterdam is, on the whole, expensive. But if you listen to me and pay attention to this chapter I promise you a full belly at the best price.

If you're on the tightest budget, head to the markets for the cheapest fruit, veggies, and cheese. I've listed several in the shopping chapter. For dry goods go to the large supermarkets and remember to bring your own bags.

If you've got access to a kitchen you might want to visit a *tropische winkel* (tropical shop) for inspiration. They're found throughout the city, especially near the markets, and they specialize in foods from tropical countries: everything from mangoes to hot sauce to cassava chips.

SUPERMARKETS

Supermarkets in Amsterdam are now open much longer hours than they used to be (in general: mon-sat 9-20; thurs 'til 21). More and more are staying open on Sundays, too. If you shop at Albert Heijn pick up a free, plastic "bonus card". You'll need it to buy anything on sale: without it you'll be charged the full price. Fill a name and address in on the form they issue at the front counter (where they sell film) and they'll give you a card right away. Anyone can use it - just give it to the cashier every time you check out.

Aldi - *Nieuwe Weteringstraat 26*
> This is one of the cheapest, but they don't have as good a selection as the bigger chains. And it's a bit hard to find. And it's kind of grungy. (Map area C8)

Dirk van den Broek
> Another cheapie, and they're starting to stock a few organic products.
> *Heinekenplein* - Big. American-style. Behind the Heineken Brewery. (Map area D8)
> *Waterlooplein 131* - Right next to the flea market. Open Sunday. (Map area E6)
> *Lijnbaansgracht 33* - In the Jordaan. (Map area B3)

Super de Boer
> Here are a few locations of this west-side chain.
> *Elandsgracht 118* - In the Jordaan. (Map area B6)
> *Rozengracht 193* - Also in the Jordaan. (Map area B5)
> *Westerstraat 100* - Again in the Jordaan. (Map area C3)

Albert Heijn
> Every time I blink there's a new one. They carry lots of organic products (look for labels marked *bio*), and the branches listed below stay open 'til 22:00 ('til 19 on sun). They're slick and well-stocked, but also expensive.
> *Nieuwezijds Voorburgwal* - Behind Dam Square. (Map area D5)
> *Koningsplein* - (Map area C6)
> *Haarlemmerdijk 1* - 10 minute walk from Central Station. (Map area C3)
> *Jodenbreestraat 20* - By the Waterlooplein flea market. (Map area E5)
> *Central Station* - In the west tunnel. Open 'til 22 on sun, too

HEALTH FOOD STORES

De Natuurwinkel - *Weteringschans 133, 638-4083 (also: Haarlemmerdijk 174; 1e Constantijn Huygensstraat 49; 1e van Swindenstraat 30)*

Health food, supermarket style. A huge selection including organic produce, cheese, and baked goods. Big, busy bulletin board. If you buy fruit or vegetables here, look for the number next to each item. Then punch in the number when you weigh it. Next push the button marked "*bon*" and a sticker will come out with the price. It's less complicated than it sounds and you won't be embarrassed at the check-out when they send you back to do it. Weteringschans branch open: mon-fri 7-20 (thurs 'til 21); sat 7-20; sun 11-18. (Map area D8)

De Aanzet - *Frans Hals Straat 27, 673-3415*

This pretty, cooperatively-run store is not far from the Albert Cuyp market (see Markets, Shopping chapter). They stock some bulk products, organic fruits and veggies, and yummy baked goods. Open: mon-fri 9-18; sat 9-17.

De Bast - Huidenstraat 19; 624-8087

Located on a street full of cute shops and restaurants, De Bast carries a selection of whole grain breads as well as all the other healthy stuff. Open: mon 11:30-18:30; tues-fri 9:30-18:30; sat 9-17. (Map area C6)

Weegschaal - *Jodenbreestraat 20, 624-1765*

You'll find all kinds of delicious, healthy foods in this neighbourhood store: from macrobiotic products, to organic fruit and veggies, to taco chips. The people who work here are very friendly. It's just around the corner from the Waterlooplein market (see Shopping chapter). Open: mon-fri 9-18; sat 9-17. (Map area E6)

De Belly - *Nieuwe Leliestraat 174, 330-9483*

A sweet, well laid out shop that's been in business for almost 30 years! It's just a few doors down from the veggie restaurant Vliegende Schotel (see Restaurants, below). Open: mon-fri 8:30-18:30; sat 8:30-17:30. (Map area B4)

't Zonnemeer - *Nieuwe Kerkstraat 8, 625-1223*

This is a small, but pleasant shop with all kinds of healthy foods. They're just a stone's throw away from the beautiful "Skinny Bridge". Open: mon-fri 8:30-18; sat 8:30-17. (Map area E7)

Natura Oase - *Jan Pieter Heijestraat 105, 618-2887*

If you're in Vondelpark and you need some picnic fixin's, stop by this neighbourhood health food store. Bring an empty bottle because they also have organic wine on tap. Open: mon-fri 8-18; sat 8-17.

STREET FOOD

Scattered all around the city are **falafel & shoarma** take-aways, where prices start at ƒ4.50 to ƒ6. For shoarma try the Damstraat (just east of Dam Square), where there's a whole row of these places. Make sure you specify "small" if that's what you want or they'll try to give you a large and embarrass you into paying for it. For the best deal on falafels go to Falafel Dan (see Restaurants, this chapter), or Maoz Falafel (Reguliersbreestraat 41, by Rembrandtplein; Leidsestraat 85). They give you the pita and falafel balls and you help yourself to the rest. All you can pile on for ƒ6. Burp!

For **french fries** ("chips" to you Brits) try any place that advertises *vlaamse frites* (Flemish fries). These are the best. There is a large choice of toppings, but get mayonnaise for the Dutch experience. There's one at Damrak 42. There's also a good one on the Korte Leidsedwarsstraat north of Leidsestraat (near Leidseplein) and, maybe the best of all, at Voetboogstraat 33 (which runs parallel to the Kalverstraat). A small is usually ƒ2.50, plus ƒ.50 each for a big selection of sauces. Delicious.

Healthy fast food is almost unheard of in Amsterdam, so this place is a find. Shakies (Central Station - west tunnel, 636-9836) makes great **juices and shakes**. All the fruit is freshly squeezed and the milk and yoghurt are organic. If you're vegan or lactose intollerent, they even have soyamilk. Prices range from ƒ3.75 to ƒ6.75, and for an extra guilder they'll throw in a shot of vitamin B, ginseng, or guarana. Also on the menu are veggie samosas, tofu rolls, and herbal teas. Not bad for a food outlet in a train station. Open: daily 7-21.

Fish lovers should definitely try snacking at one of the herring stalls that are all over the city. They're easily recognizable by their fish flags. All kinds of **fish and seafood** sandwiches are available from ƒ2.75. There is one close to Central Station on the bridge where the Haarlemmerstraat crosses the Singel canal and another next to the Westerkerk. Or for authentic British - read "extremely greasy" - fish and chips, try Al's at Nieuwendijk 10.

Another good bet for cheap food is **Indonesian or Surinamese** take-away. A big roti meal will cost you about ƒ7 to ƒ9. A large plate of fried rice with chicken and pork runs about ƒ9 to ƒ10 and is often enough for two people. For the best deal, though, see Restaurants, this chapter.

For relatively cheap **Chinese** take-away look around the Zeedijk (off of Nieuwmarkt) where there's a small Chinatown. And at the markets don't forget to try the cheap and addictive Vietnamese *Loempias* (spring rolls): veggie or chicken, ƒ1 to ƒ1.50.

Febo is the name of a chain of gross automats that you'll see all over the city. Here you can get **greasy**, deep-fried snacks for a couple of guilders. In my opinion, your best bet is the *kaas* (cheese) *soufflé*. Here are a few locations: Damrak 6 (just down from Central Station); Kalverstraat 142; Nieuwendijk 220. They're open every night 'til 3.

While I generally hate American franchises, I was very happy to see Ben & Jerry's open in Amsterdam (Leidsestraat 90, and platform 1 in Central Station), especially since once a year, in the spring, they have their annual Global Free Cone Day (see the Get Lost! website for dates). Great **ice cream**. Leidsestraat shop open: daily 11-1:00 in summer; wed-sun 11-18 in winter.

Pizza slices in Amsterdam were my idea, damn it, and now they're everywhere. When they're fresh, New York Pizza (*Leidsestraat 23; Spui 2; Damstraat 24*) has the best slices in town. Prices range from ƒ4 to ƒ5.50.

NIGHT SHOPS

"Night Shops" are the only places to buy groceries after the supermarkets close and are accordingly expensive. Fruit and veggies at these shops are a rip-off, but all the usual junk foods are available. Most night shops are open daily from 16:00 to 1:00. After that, you're fucked. However, a new law may soon license some to stay open all night. Here are a few in the centre.

Pinguin Nightshop - *Berenstraat 5. Between the Prinsengracht and the Keizersgracht.* (Map area C5)

Big Bananas - *Leidsestraat 73.* This night shop does a lot of business because of its location, but what a grumpy bunch. (Map area C6)

Avondmarkt - *de Wittenkade 94.* West end. The best selection and prices. (Map B2)

Sterk - *Waterlooplein 241.* This place has cold-cuts, salads and cheeses too. (Map E6)

Baltus T - *Vijzelstraat 127.* (Map area D7)

Dolf - *Willemsstraat 79.* In the Jordaan. (Map area C2)

Texaco - *Sarphatistraat 225; Marnixstraat 250.* Open 24 hours. Eat here and get gas. (Map areas H6, B5)

ALL NIGHT EATING

De Prins - *Weteringschans 1*

Situated right across the street from the Paradiso (see Music chapter). Open: sun-thurs 'til 3; fri/sat 'til 4. (Map area C7)

Bojo - *Lange Leidsedwarsstraat 51*

This Indonesian restaurant (see Restaurants in this chapter) is open Saturday and Sunday until 4 and weeknights until 2. It's a good place for a late night pig-out. (Map area C7)

Gary's Late Nite - *Reguliersdwarsstraat 53, 420-2406*

Visit this little shop (see Cafés), in the wee hours for muffins, cookies, and bagels. Open: sun-thurs 'til 3; fri/sat 'til 4. (Map area D6)

easyEverything - Damrak 33, Reguliersbreestraat 22,

There's not a big selection of eats - pre-packaged cake, sandwiches, that kind of stuff - at this internet café (see Hanging Out chapter), but in the middle of the night in Amsterdam, you can't be too choosy. Open: daily 24 hours. (Map area D4, D6)

Febo Snackbars - *all over*

I can't really recommend this shit, but they're open late and they're cheap (see Street Food in this chapter). Do what you gotta do.

New York Pizza - *Leidsestraat 23, Damstraat 24*

Pizza slices until 1 on weekdays and 4 on weekends. (see Street Food, above)

BREAD

Bakker Arend - *Plantage Doklaan 8*

Once a week, this squat fills with the delicious smell of fresh bread made with organic ingredients. Also on offer are fantastic pizzas, cookies, tarts, and other yummy stuff. When you enter the building, the bakery is through the first door on the left. There are a couple of little tables if you want to have something there with a cup of tea, soup, or organic elderberry wine. Open: wed 16-21. (Map area F6)

Le Marché - *Kalverstraat 201; Rokin 160*

Some of the best bread in town. Open: mon-sat 10-19 (thurs 'til 21); sun 12-18. (Map area D6)

Bakery Paul Anée - *Runstraat 25, 623-5322; Bellamystraat 2, 618-3113*

Exclusively hearty, healthy baked goods are sold at this famous bakery. I know people who are addicted to their muesli rolls. They also sell almond and cashew butter. Open: mon-fri 9-18; sat 9-17. (Map area C5)

FREE SAMPLES

I don't know how desperate you are but...

Stalls at the Organic Farmers' Market (see Shopping) are a great source of free samples. Some Albert Heijn supermarkets have free coffee - usually by the deli counter. Gary's Muffin's (see Cafés) sometimes have one or two baskets on the counter with samples of their goodies. And finally, it's not food, but the Body Shop (Kalverstraat 157) displays tester bottles of all their lotions, creams and perfumes. Just because you're travelling doesn't mean you should let yourself go.

BREAKFAST

Breakfast is such a good meal, but if you're travelling on a budget you don't want to be forking out a lot of dough - especially so early in the day. If you can't find a hotel that includes breakfast (see Hotels, Places to Sleep chapter), then here is a selection of eating spots where you can get something for less than ƒ15.

For the record, an *uitsmijter* (pronounced "outsmyter") means bouncer, and it's what you serve your guests late at night just before you kick them out of your flat. It consists of an egg fried with cheese, ham or another meat and slipped onto a piece of toast. It's very Dutch.

Finally, before you order coffee please read the introduction to the Cafés chapter in this book. It might save your life (or at least ƒ2.50).

Barney's Breakfast Bar - *Haarlemmerstraat 102, 625-9761*
http://www.barneys-amsterdam.com

Psssst. This is also a coffeeshop so you can get stoned while you munch. English is happily spoken and b-fast is served all day. Three scrambled eggs on toast is ƒ13.50. Pancakes are ƒ12.50. Coffee is served in a big cup. The music is played a bit too loud, but it's a pleasant atmosphere nonetheless. It's located on an interesting shopping street. Open: daily, 7-20 in summer; 8-20 in winter. (Map area D3)

Winkel Lunchcafe - *Noordermarkt 43, 623-0223*

If you're visiting one of the markets by the Noorderkerk on Saturday or Monday morning (see Markets, Shopping chapter) be sure to stop in at this very popular café on the corner of the square. They serve one of the best apple cakes in Amsterdam. Everyone gets a piece and sits outside drinking cappuccino or fresh orange juice at shared tables along the crowded Westerstraat. It costs ƒ5, but the slices are big and you'll feel stuffed. Open: mon-sat 7-18. (Map area C3)

Dimitri's Café - *Prinsenstraat 3, 627-9393*

Dimitri's is located on a very pretty street between two canals. It's a comfortable place to drink a pot of tea (ƒ3.50) and read the paper while you wait for your breakfast. They've got yoghurt and muesli for ƒ5.75, and until noon you can get a big breakfast for ƒ10.50. If it's too crowded, try Vennington, the little place across the street which is also great. Open: daily 8-22. (Map area C3)

De Peper - *Overtoom 301, 779-4912*

If you have a wild Saturday night and wake up late, plop yourself onto a couch at this squat restaurant (see below), listen to some tunes, and grab a late breakfast. Last time I was there they were serving a black-bean paté with a big salad, all made with organic produce. It wasn't gourmet, but it was only ƒ5! Open: sun 12-17. (Map area A7)

Lunchlokaal Wynand Fockink - *Pijlsteeg 31, 639-2695*

It's not super cheap, but this cute little café (see Cafés) offers a breakfast special from 10 to 11:00: two sandwiches (ham or cheese), orange juice, a boiled egg, and coffee for ƒ14,50. Open: daily 10-18 (closed mon, oct - apr). (Map area D5)

RESTAURANTS

Warung Mini - *Ceintuurbaan 205, 662-6804*

Surinamese/Indonesian. It's a bit out of the centre, but what a deal! Warung Mini serves up big, wonderful meals starting at only ƒ7.50 for a vegetarian or chicken roti (curried veggies, egg, and a roti). There are also lots of rice and noodle dishes in the ƒ10 range, and soups for ƒ5. For dessert try a "baked banana" - deep fried banana strips in a batter. Oh yeah. Open: mon-sat 11-23; sun 12-23.

Albert Cuyp 67 - *Albert Cuyp 67, 671-1396*

Surinamese/Chinese. This little restaurant lies between two others that have basically the same menu, which in turn is similar to that of Warung Mini (above). Big portions for a low price. They have a chicken roti for only *f*7! There are plenty of choices for vegetarians too. Meals run from *f*7 to *f*13 and don't be shy to ask what's what. Excellent banana chips. Located near the Albert Cuyp market (see Markets, Shopping chapter). Open: daily 12-22:30.

Vliegende Schotel (Flying Saucer) - *Nieuwe Leliestraat 162, 625-2041*

Vegetarian. This restaurant is situated in a beautiful neighbourhood called the Jordaan (pronounced "yordahn"), so make sure that you take a walk around before or after your meal. They have a big menu that includes some vegan dishes. Meals start at *f*12.50, and half-servings from *f*7.50. Soup of the day is *f*5.50. Order at the back and leave your name. They'll run a tab for you and you pay as you leave. It's comfy and friendly inside, and the room on the left is non-smoking. The only problem here is that the service is very slow and they often run out of food. If you're in a hurry or are very hungry, make sure you show up early. Open daily from 17:30 to 23:30, but the last call for dinner orders is at 22:15. (Map area B4)

Thaise Snack bar Bird - *Zeedijk 77, 420-6289*

Thai. If you've ever been to Thailand you'll like this place. It's got the atmosphere down pat, with Thai pop songs, pictures of the king, and orchids on the tables. A lot of Thai people eat here, which is a good sign of authentic cooking. Meals aren't super cheap (average *f*17), but the food is always prepared fresh and it's delicious. Worth the walk through this sleazy, junkie-filled neighbourhood. Open: daily 15-22. (Map area E4)

Raan Phad Thai - *Kloveniersburgwal 18, 420-0665*

Thai. If Bird is too crowded, this friendly place is just a short walk up the street. There are only a few tables inside, under an old beamed ceiling, and the window offers a nice view of the canal. Prices range from *f*13.50 for a Thai curry with rice, to *f*21.50 for fried noodles with shrimp. Open daily, mar-nov 13-21; in winter 15-21. (Map E5)

Kam Yin - *Warmoesstraat 6, 625-3115*

Surinamese/Chinese. The best food of this type (at the right price) in the centre of Amsterdam. They have a big menu of rice and noodle items and the servings are huge. Dishes start at about *f*8.50 and one main dish along with a side order is probably enough for two people. Eat-in or take-away. Two minutes from Central Station. Open: daily 12-24. (Map area E4)

Falafel Dan - *Ferdinand Bolstraat 126, 676-3411*

Falafel. Actually, they serve more than falafels here, but that's what I go for. *f*6 buys you a pita full of delicious, freshly-prepared falafel balls. Then you waltz over to the salad and sauce bar and cram as much as you can into the pita. For me, it's a meal. And get this, every day from 15 to 17:00 is happy hour: all you can eat falafel balls! They also have a great selection of fresh juices. It's located near the Albert Cuyp market and has seating in the back. Open: mon-thurs 12-1; fri/sat 12-3; sun 13-1.

Addis Ababa - *Overtoom 337, 618-4472*

Ethiopian. This is a great restaurant to go to with a bunch of friends. The food is served in the traditional way, on a giant platter, and everyone eats with their hands. The decor is lively and the owner is a really nice guy. There are several veggie dishes, and something for carnivores, too. A full meal and a drink will set you back about ƒ15 per person - not exactly cheap, but not expensive either. Open: daily 17-23:00. (Map area A7)

Foodism - *Oude Leliestraat 8, 427-5103*

Everything. This funky little restaurant is on the same pretty street as Grey Area (see Coffeeshops, Cannabis chapter). They make wonderful soups, salads, sandwiches, and a delicious vegetarian pasta. It's also a nice place to have a leisurely brunch with some friends. Although it's open for dinner, I actually prefer it earlier in the day before it gets too smoky. Open: daily 10:30-22:00. (Map area C4)

De Peper - *Overtoom 301, 779-4912*
http://www.contrast.org/peper

Organic Vegan. After sitting empty for some time, this former film school was squatted. It now houses several studios, a movie theatre (see Film chapter) living spaces, and a great restaurant called De Peper. It's very popular so make sure you call ahead or arrive when they open in order to reserve a meal. Find out how long you'll have to wait and then kick back with an organic beer or juice. The meal consists of a starter (usually soup) and a lovingly prepared main course. The ƒ10 price is cheap for healthy, vegan food. Dessert costs an extra ƒ2.50. They cook three nights a week. The bar stays open late and sometimes there are parties and performances after dinner. From Leidseplein it's about a 10 minute walk, or you can hop on tram 1. Open: tues, fri, sun 18-23. (Map area A7)

Soup En Zo - *Jodenbreestraat 94a, 422-2243*

Soup. In a welcome addition to Amsterdam's culinary scene, the concept of the soup stall has arrived. The cooks in this little restaurant use fresh, often organically-grown vegetables in their soups. And there are always several choices for vegetarians. It's not super cheap (averaging ƒ6 to ƒ8 for a bowl), but the soups really are delicious, and in nice weather there are tables out front. Soup En Zo is located close by the Waterlooplein market and just a few doors down from the anarchist bookstore, Het Fort van Sjakoo (see Books, Shopping chapter). Open: mon-sat 11-20; sun 13-19. (Map area E6)

La Place Grand Café Restaurant - *Kalverstraat 201, Rokin 160, 622-0171*

Everything. Occupying a couple of little seventeenth-century houses, this department store food court lacks the usual fast-food crap and atmosphere. Elegant little booths display a wide variety of beautiful fresh fruits and vegetables bought directly from the producers. They also claim that most of their meat is free-range. The menu changes daily and everything is prepared fresh. Here are some of the cheaper examples from the last time I was here: gorgeous sandwiches ƒ4-5, soup ƒ5.50, excellent french fries ƒ3.75, giant hot chocolate with whipped cream ƒ2.95. It's a good place to seek refuge from the crowds of the Kalverstraat and they actually have a non-smoking section. The bakery attached to this restaurant makes some of the best bread in Amsterdam. Open: mon-sat 10-21 (thurs 'til 22); sun 12-21. (Map area D6)

Zaal 100 - *De Wittenstraat 100, 688-0127*

Vegetarian/vegan. There's all kinds of stuff going on in this building (which I think used to be a squat), but to find the food, go in the main doors and turn to your right. The first door on your right, just past the bar, is the one you want. Inside is a crowded, cosy room filled with tables and mismatched chairs. There are stairs in the hallway that lead up to a small balcony with more seating. It's perfectly acceptable to share a table if the place is busy. A full meal of soup (*f*1.50), a big plate of food for the main dish (*f*7), and dessert (*f*1.50) adds up to only *f*10. It's not a gourmet meal, but it is tasty and filling. You don't need to reserve, but you should show up early. Wednesdays are vegan. Closed in July and August. Open: tues, wed, thurs 18-20. (Map area B2)

Café de Molli - *Van Ostadestraat 55, 676-1427*

Vegetarian. This place serves up cheap, big meals every Saturday evening. Just *f*7 gets you a full veggie meal in a very basic, communal setting. Call the number above in the afternoon to reserve your meal. For a little more info about this squat see the Cafés chapter. Meals are served at 19:00. *Eet Smakelijk!*

Einde van de Wereld (End of the World) - *Javakade, KNSM Island*

Home-cooked. With a lot of hard work by volunteers, the lively atmosphere of this famous squat restaurant has been transplanted onto a boat! Step down into the hold of the ship and there's a bright, bustling room filled with great music and the smell of terrific cooking. Go early as they only serve until the food runs out. There's a choice of a vegetarian or meat dish for *f*12.50 or a half plate (lots of kids here) for *f*6. Dessert costs *f*3. It's a good deal: the servings are huge and there's also bread and garlic butter on the tables. Drinks are cheap. Order your meal at the bar, leave your name, pay, and in about 15 minutes they'll bring you your food. In good weather, take your beer and sit up top, overlooking the water. The boat's name is Quo Vadis and there's little sign in front. You can take bus 32 from Central Station eastbound (it'll say "KNSM Laan" on the front), to the Azartplein stop. Then follow the road to the left for a few minutes. Or better yet, take a bicycle. AMP is also in this area (see Live Music/Party Venues, Music chapter). Einde van de Wereld is open only on Wednesdays and Fridays from 18:00. (Map area I3)

Toscana - *Haarlemmerstraat 130, 622-0353; Haarlemmerdijk 176, 624-8358*

Italian. I'm always complaining to visitors about how pathetic Amsterdam pizzas are. And this place is no exception. But, all their pizzas are half price and I love a bargain. The cheapest pizza is a thin, but big, margherita for *f*7, which means you can have a pizza and a beer for about *f*10.50. And even though I bitch a fair bit, it's not terrible pizza. "When the moon hits your eye, like a big pizza pie, that's *amoré*..." Open: daily 16-23. (Map area C2)

Pannekoekhuis Upstairs - *Grimburgwal 2, 626-5603*

Pancakes. Not having a pancake in Holland would be like coming here and not seeing a windmill. It's part of the Dutch experience. This tiny place is on the second floor of a very cute, very old house. They have an English menu with prices starting at about *f*6 for a powdered sugar topping. A pancake with strawberries and whipped cream goes for *f*10.50. Students get a 10% discount. Open: mar-oct, tues-sun 12-19. In winter: wed-fri 12-19; sat 12-18; sun 12-17. Closed in January. (Map area D5)

Bojo - *Lange Leidsedwarsstraat 51, 626-8990*
Indonesian. This place is in all the tourist guides, but a lot of Dutch people go here too because the servings are huge, the prices are reasonable (ƒ13 to ƒ18), and they're open late. Skip the appetizers: they're not very good. They also have a stupid rule that if you sit outside they won't give you a glass of water. The food is pretty good here, but if you want a real Indonesian "rice table" (and they're excellent) you have to pay at least ƒ40 per person. If you have the dough try "Cilubang" (Runstraat 10, 626-9755) where the food is fantastic. Bojo is open: mon-thurs 16-2; fri 16-4; sat 12-4; sun 12-2. (Map area C7)

The Fridge - *Frederick Hendrikstraat 111, 684-6437*
Vegetarian. With the beats of different DJs to inspire them, the organizers of this very cool restaurant whip up delicious, healthy food two nights a week. The filling dinners cost ƒ10 and start with soup (which the cooks are particularly good at concocting). Then a main dish is served and, for an extra ƒ2.50, dessert. There's no menu - if they feel like cooking Japanese, or Indian, or Mexican, then that's what they cook. You never know until you get there. The bar stays open later if you want to hang out for awhile and listen to the tunes. Open: wed, thurs from 19. (Map area A4)

Fine dining at the Fridge

The Atrium - *Oudezijds Achterburgwal 237, 525-3999*
Cafeteria food. This is a self-service student mensa with cheap meals from about ƒ7 to ƒ9 (even cheaper for students). Outside of meal times it's also a pleasant place to grab an inexpensive cup of coffee and a croissant and to rest your feet a bit. Meals are served on weekdays from 12 to 14:00 and 17 to 19:30. There's another student mensa, Agora, at Roetersstraat 13, that also offers cheap meals and a big non-smoking section. Same hours as the Atrium. (Map area D5)

Mafaldo - *Kinkerstraat 338, 683-9105*
Algerian / Mediterranean. If you find yourself out in this part of town (it's just around the corner from the Kashmir Lounge - see Coffeeshops, Cannabis chaptér), stop in at this little Algerian place for some excellent food. The owner makes delicious couscous starting at ƒ10. The balls in the falafels (ƒ6) are made fresh, with a perfect amount of garlic in them, and the lentil soup (ƒ6) is spiced just right. You can eat at one of the little tables or get it to go. A few doors down is Kismet, a well-known Turkish bakery that also cooks up meals for ƒ10. Mafaldo is open: mon 14:30-22; tues-sat 12-22; sun 16-22.

Keuken van 1870 - *Spuistraat 4, 624 8965*

Cafeteria food. It opened as a soup kitchen in 1870, and you can still get a very cheap meal here. Full course, meat-and-potato dishes go for only ƒ10. Soup of the day is ƒ3.50. It's close to Central Station. Open: mon-fri 12-20; sat 16-21. (Map area D3)

Hap-Hmm - *1st Helmersstraat 33; 618-1884*

Dutch food. Just like dinner in mom's kitchen. Hap-Hmm is a little eatery located on a residential street that runs parallel to the Overtoom. They serve a lot of meat dishes, but there's also always a selection of vegetables, and lately they've been adding different sorts of veggie and tofu burgers to the menu, too. The set menus start at ƒ10.50, salads go for ƒ2.75, and soup-of-the-day is ƒ2.50. It's nothing fancy, but it's a good price for a filling Dutch meal in a homey environment. Expect the other diners to be old folk from the neighbourhood, and other people with *Get Lost!*. Open: sun-fri 16:30-20. (Map area 7B)

Moeder's Pot - *Vinkenstraat 119, 623-7643*

Dutch food. It may be called Mother's Pot, but it's really Pop's Grill. Except for the kitchen, Pop doesn't keep the little place too clean, and it has an atmosphere of neglect. The food, however, is tasty and plentiful. Generous servings of authentic Dutch meat-and-potato dishes can be had for less than ƒ10. The vegetable plate (*not* suitable for vegetarians) is a great deal at ƒ7.50, especially if you're tired and hungry after a long day. Open: mon-sat 17-22. (Map area C2)

Restaurant de Hemelvaart - Oude Haagseweg 58, 669-2513
http://www.rijkshemelvaart.com

Vegetarian. Way the hell out by the Amsterdamse Bos (see Parks, Hanging Out chapter), in an old military compound that was squatted in 1989, a small group of people have created a "free state" in which to live and work. One of the several projects going on at the site is a vegetarian restaurant that's open most summers in one form or another. In the past they've combined meals with DJs, films, and video re-runs of *The Love Boat*. The generous servings of whatever food they cook up usually runs about ƒ12.50. If the weather is good, you can eat outside. Call first to make sure they're open and to make a reservation. Then make a day of it by riding out to the Bos before you eat. Otherwise you can take tram 2 to the second last stop, after which it's about a 10-minute walk. Open Saturdays in the summer from 18:30.

CAFÉS

Cafés are plentiful in Amsterdam, and they're ideal places to hang out and get a feel for the city. Once you've ordered you'll be left alone to read or write postcards or vegetate for as long as you like. Don't be shy to ask to share a table if you see a free chair: this is one of the most densely populated countries in the world (16 million people) and table sharing is customary.

Koffie verkeerd (literally "incorrect coffee") is *café au lait* and if you order "ordinary coffee" you'll probably get an espresso. Tea is charged by the cup and extra water will be added to your bill. I don't know the reason for this dumb custom. Fresh-squeezed orange juice, which is commonly referred to in french - *jus d'orange* - is available in most cafés.

Many cafés also serve snacks such as *broodjes* (small sandwiches) and *tostis* (usually ham and cheese sandwiches squashed into a sandwich toaster). Prices start at about *f*3 for a plain cheese-on-white-roll or tosti. Another popular item is apple cake with whipped cream. It's an incredibly delicious Amsterdam speciality that should definitely be experienced.

For internet cafés, see the Hanging Out chapter.

Café Latei - *Zeedijk 143, 625-7485*

Do you ever wake up and think to yourself, "I feel like drinking a cup of coffee, then buying some organic olive oil and a piece of furniture"? Because this cute, split-level café's got all that and more. Almost everything in here is for sale: the chair you're sitting on, Finnish wallpaper, knick-knacks, and a variety of olive oils. The way everything is scattered about here creates the sensation that you're in someone's living room. It's a great little place to pop into for a fresh-squeezed juice and a big bowl of soup with bread. Open: mon-thurs 8-19; fri 8-22; sat 9-22; sun 11-19. (Map area E4)

Villa Zeezicht - *Torensteeg 7*

Even with their expansion into the shop next door, this remains a cosy café. The seats by the big windows are perfect for reading the paper and people-watching. In the summer there are tables outside and on the bridge. Sandwiches are *f*4 to *f*6. They also make an awesome apple cake for *f*5 (a meal in itself). Make sure to ask for whipped cream (*f*1). Open: mon-fri 8-18:30; sat/sun 9-18:30. (Map area D4)

Café ter Kuile - *Torensteeg 8, 639-1055*

This pretty café/bar gets very crowded in the day with students from the university. But at night, after the dinner hour, it becomes mellower. I'm talking candles on the table, Tom Waits on the stereo, and a warm buzz of conversation. It's a good place to shoot the shit with a friend. Open: daily 11-1; fri/sat 'til 3. (Map area D4)

Backstage Boutique and Coffee-Corner - *Utrechtsedwarsstraat 67, 622-3638*

Greg, one of the Christmas Twins (identical twins who were big stars back in the US), died not long ago, and he is missed by many, many people. But his brother

Gary is still running the Peewee-esque café they built together, and its unique atmosphere endures. It's not really cheap, but this place is great! They serve coffees, teas, juices and an assortment of sandwiches and cakes. The bottom of the menu proclaims: "Mama wanted girls!" The walls are decorated with wild sweaters and hats that were designed and made by the twins. If you're lucky, you might even walk out with a souvenir postcard. Gary is super friendly and very funny. Open: mon-sat 10-18. (Map area E7)

Café Vertigo - *Vondelpark 3, 612-3021*
http://www.vertigo

This café has one of the nicest (and busiest) terraces in Amsterdam. It's located in the middle of Vondelpark in the Film Museum building (see Film chapter). In bad weather duck into the cosy, low-ceilinged café. On Saturday nights they have DJs. Sometimes there are slide shows at the back. Open: daily 11-1 (from 10 in spring and summer). (Map area B8)

Greenwoods - *Singel 103, 623-7071*

An Australian opened this café almost 13 years ago and despite the fact that it's trendy, I still like it. It gets very crowded around lunch, but at other times it's a calm place to have some tea and a bite to eat. There aren't many places in A'dam where you can get a pot of tea (ƒ4.50). They also have bagels with cream cheese, tomato and lettuce (ƒ4.50), and a selection of home-baked cakes and scones. Open: daily 9:30-19. (Map area D4)

Tofani - *Kloveniersburgwal 20*

There's nothing pretentious about this Italian shop near the Nieuwmarkt. It's an old-school joint selling great sandwiches and wonderful gelati. Five different sandwiches are served on panini bread. A mozzarella, lettuce, tomato and basil goes for ƒ6.75. There are also hot sandwiches. Order at the counter and have a seat at one of the tables outside. They'll tap on the window when it's ready. It's perfect for a fast lunch, especially when the weather is nice. Gelati starts at ƒ1.50 for one ball. Open from March until the end of October.

De Tuin - *2e Tuindwarsstraat 13, 624-4559*

De Tuin is a spacious, inviting café right in the heart of a beautiful old neighbourhood called the Jordaan. It's a traditional "brown café" (so-called because of the abundance of wood). I like to explore the area and then pop in here for an orange juice and a sandwich. There are usually cool people hanging out and it's a comfortable spot to relax for awhile. The view of the Westerkerk tower from this shopping street is particularly photogenic. Open: mon-thurs 10-1; fri/sat 10-2; sun 11-1. (Map area B3)

Bagels & Beans - *Ferdinand Bolstraat 70, 672-1610; Keisersgracht 504*
http://www.bagelsbeans.nl

The bagels here, for my money, are the best in Amsterdam. They're often served hot out of the oven. A plain bagel costs ƒ1.50; with cream cheese, ƒ3.50. If you've got ƒ10 you can splurge on a litre of Ben and Jerry's ice cream (hey, you're not in Vermont anymore, Dorothy). They serve delicious coffees too, but I can't handle the thick tobacco smoke that engulfs everything here, so unless their terrace is set up, I usually get something to go. Open: mon-fri 8:30-18; sat 10-18; sun 10-18:00.

Café de Pels - *Huidenstraat 25, 622-9037*

This is another traditional "brown café" with a diverse clientele. It's warm and welcoming in the winter, while in the summer the tiny outdoor tables make for good people-watching on this quaint little street. It has an authentic Amsterdam ambiance. Open: mon-thurs 10-1; fri/sat 10-3; sun 11-1. (Map area C5)

Gary's Muffins - *Prinsengracht 454, 420-1452; Marnixstraat 121, 638-0186; Reguliers-dwarsstraat 53, 420-2406; Jodenbreestraat 15, 421-5930; Kinkerstraat 140, 412-3025*

Muffin's, brownies, cookies and yes, bagels. Though I'm not crazy about Gary's baked goods, I still stop in sometimes for a big chocolate chip cookie (ƒ3), and a bagel with cream cheese (ƒ4.75). They also serve organic, fair-trade coffee. The Prinsengracht and Jodenbreestraat locations have tables outside in the summer. Otherwise, I go to Marnixstaat which is airier and more comfortable inside. Usually you can pick up day-olds for ƒ1.50. Gary's Late Night on Reguliersdwarstraat is open during the day, but I often swing by when I've got the munchies in the middle of the night. The shops each have their own opening times, but it's generally mon-sat 8:30-18; sun 10-18. Gary's Late Night is open: sun-thurs 12-3; fri/sat 12-4.

De Ruimte - *Eerste Constantijn Huygenstraat 20, 427-5951*
http://www.smartprojectspace.net

The Smart Project Space was created by a network of artists to enable and promote contemporary (particularly new-media) art. The café/restaurant De Ruimte is part of the project. While debate over the future of the building continues, it'll be used for exhibitions, films, and other activities. During the day the atmosphere in the café is hip, yet super-mellow. Drinks aren't cheap, but I like to drop in here to kick back for a bit and listen to some jazz before wandering through the exhibition space. At night, the restaurant gets very crowded with a trendy crowd. Open: tues-sun midday-late.

Lunchlokaal Wynand Fockink - *Pijlsteeg 31, 639-2695*

The quaint little courtyard where this café is located provides respite from the bustle of the Dam Square area. In the winter it's just a nice little hideaway. In the summer though, the trees and plants grow lush around the little tables, creating a wonderfully peaceful environment. It's not super cheap, but they have sandwiches from ƒ5.50, and soup of the day with bread for ƒ5. Between 10 and 11:00 you can get breakfast for ƒ14,50 (see Breakfast, Food section). Go through the covered walkway by Leonida's chocolates on Damstraat and you'll find it. Open: daily 10-18 (closed mon oct - apr). (Map area D5)

The Meeting Point (COC) - *Rozenstraat 14, 626-3087*
http://www.cocamsterdam.nl

This café is in the home of Amsterdam's main gay and lesbian resource centre (founded over 50 years ago!). Its relaxed atmosphere and (usually) considerate volunteer staff make this a good spot to have a drink and find out about gay happenings in Amsterdam. Pick up a copy of *Shark*, a free, bi-weekly listing of what's going on around town. The free English- and Dutch-language paper *Gay News* is also available here. On Friday nights the COC hosts a mixed dance, and there's a women-only dance every Saturday night (from 22:00; admission ƒ5). The café is currently open: fri/sat 13-17; and maybe more days in the future. (Map area C4)

Café de Molli - *Van Ostadestraat 55, 676-1427*

This is a volunteer-run squat café with an emphasis on politics. They frequently host theme nights with videos and speakers on subjects such as the role of Shell (those murdering motherfuckers) in Nigeria. On other nights it's just a mellow place to hang out and meet some people. Drinks are very cheap. Tea is free. They also have a feminist café every second Wednesday of the month where a vegetarian meal is served. Open: sun-fri 21-1; sat for dinner only (see Restaurants, Food chapter).

W139 - *Warmoesstraat 139, 622-9434*
http://www.W139.nl

This building, which was squatted a while back, has been turned into an art gallery. The space is huge - perfect for the regularly changing, multi-media exhibitions on display. There's no charge to visit. The café, when it's open, is a cool, if somewhat grungy, place to kick back for a bit before heading back out into the crowds of the city centre. It's best to go in the summer, though, as it gets quite cold inside in the winter. Tea and coffee are cheap, and they also serve wine and malt beer. Open: wed-sun 13-18:00. (Map area D4)

De Jaren - *Nieuwe Doelenstraat 20, 625-5771*
http://cafe-de-jaren.nl

I find the food overpriced here, but I like the spaciousness, which is unusual in this city and means that you can almost always find a seat. In the summer there are two big terraces with a terrific view over the Amstel River. It's right by the university and lots of intellectuals hang out here reading books. I often stop in to use the toilet. Located between Waterlooplein and Rembrandtplein. Open: sun-thurs 10-1; fri/sat 10-2. (Map area D6)

Manege - *Vondelstraat 140, 618-0942*

I'd always heard that this horse riding school had a great café with cheap drinks and snacks. It's true. Vondelstraat runs alongside Vondelpark (see Parks, Hanging Out chapter). Walk through the arch under the huge lamps, and enter the school via the big doors. The café is through the door on the left, and up a grandiose stairway. There's a balcony with tables overlooking the training area, but if you find the horsey aroma a bit much, you can still see through the windows of the main room of the café. It was formerly very elegant and is now filled with cats. If you're coming from the park, take the exit near the Film Museum. Open: mon-fri 10-24; sat 10-17; sun 10-16. (Map area A7)

De Badcuyp - *1e Sweelinckstraat 10, 675-9669*
http://www.badcuyp.demon.nl

This former bathhouse was saved from demolition by activists in the neighbourhood. Now it's a "centre for art, culture and politics" that's partly run by volunteers. It's located in the middle of the crowded Albert Cuyp Market (see Markets, Shopping chapter), and in nice weather there are tables outside. Inside it's spacious and relaxed: newspapers are scattered around and art exhibits line the walls. The upper level gives you a good view of the last-minute shoppers in the market below. They have a bar that serves snacks and full meals (the meal of the day costs ƒ14.50). There's often live music, either in the café or in the hall upstairs where they also host popular dance nights featuring salsa, funk, jazz and disco. Open: tues-thurs 17-1; fri/sat 17-3; sun 17-1. (Map area E8)

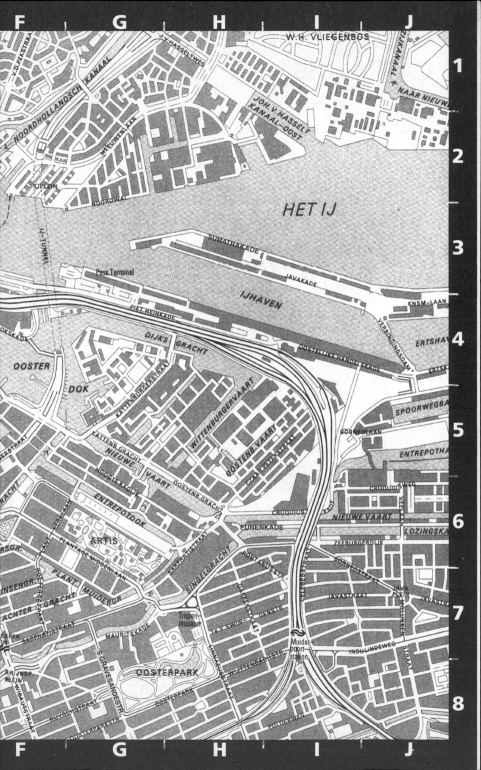

CANNABIS

If you like to smoke marijuana and hash, and come from anywhere other than the Parvati Valley, then you're in for a treat. In Amsterdam you can walk into any "coffeeshop" (a café selling grass and hash) and order a coffee and a joint; then sit back and smoke, listen to music, perhaps have a game of backgammon or chess - without the worry of being arrested. How civilized!
You don't have to buy weed every time you go into a coffeeshop, but definitely buy something: a drink or some munchies.

The weed here is probably a lot stronger than what you're used to back home. If you find that a friend of yours is too high or feels a bit sick, often a sweet drink (like a cola) will help. Just thought I'd mention that.

Almost all coffeeshops have a menu listing the types of smoke available and where each one is from. It's fun to try grass from different parts of the world, but I have to say that a lot of the *nederwiet* (Dutch grown weed) is spectacular. Prices are usually listed by the gram and the weed is often sold in ƒ10 or ƒ25 bags. So if, for instance, Haze #1 is selling for ƒ16 a gram, a ƒ10 bag will contain 0.6 grams. Some coffeeshops will let you buy smaller amounts, too. Don't be shy to ask to see the menu: it's there to make it easy for you. Some strains are listed as "*hydro*" meaning that it was grown hydroponically. Others are listed as "*bio*", meaning it was grown in soil. This doesn't mean it was grown organically as is the case with products marked *bio* in grocery stores. However, many coffeeshops are starting to sell organically grown weed. It's no problem to ask to see the buds before you pay. Then relax while you roll and ponder the absurdity of North America's repressive and hypocritical "war on drugs", and how fantastic it is to be in Amsterdam!

Attention: Don't buy anything on the street! You will definitely be ripped off!

Warning: Space cakes and *bon bons* (containing grass or hash) are sold in some coffee shops. They can be very strong, almost like tripping, so have fun, but be prepared for a long, intense high. Also keep in mind that they can take up to a couple of hours to kick in, so don't gobble down another one just because you don't feel anything right away................................. What?

COFFEESHOPS

Grey Area - *Oude Leliestraat 2, 420-4301*
http://www.greyarea.nl

Originally, this coffeeshop was Amsterdam's first hempseed restaurant. Now they only serve tasty morsels of the smokable kind. They have a very select menu offering some of the newest strains of weed around, yet despite this exclusivity, their prices are very reasonable. Connoisseurs will definitely get a kick out of this place. The staff are friendly and welcoming, the little old street it's on is beautiful, and the organic coffee is served in a bottomless cup! Play the game on their website and you get a printable coupon you can bring with you for a free drink. Open: tues-sun 12-20. (Map area C4)

Global Chillage - *Kerkstraat 51, 777-9777*
http://www.globalchillage.com

Most nights find the low seating lining this "chill out lounge" full of stoned, happy people. The lighting, decor, and ambient music all work to create an atmosphere of, well... global chillage! They've always got friendly people working here and it's a cool place to hang out and enjoy the vibe. Open: daily 10-24. (Map C6)

Dampkring - *Handboogstraat 29, 638-0705*
http://www.dampkring.nl

The super funky decor and some killer hash and buds have made the Dampkring a longtime favourite with both locals and tourists alike. It can get pretty crowded in here, and if you're looking for a mellow experience the music can be a little loud, but otherwise it's a comfortable shop with friendly, knowledgable staff. When you get the munchies head over to the great french-fry place around the corner on Voetboogstraat (see Street Food, Shopping chapter). The same owners also have another coffeeshop called the Tweede Kamer (Heisteeg 6), a sweet little place with the same great hash. Dampkring open: mon-thurs 10-1; fri/sat 10-2; sun 11-1.

De Rokerij - *Lange Leidsedwarsstraat 41, 622-9442*
http://www.rokerij.net

Who would guess that in the middle of this touristy strip there's a great coffeeshop? The decor in here is a mixture of Amsterdam and Asian motifs. The music is spacey, but not sleepy, and there are lots of comfortable nooks to settle into. It's a popular spot and you can tell that they have a lot of regulars hanging out. My only complaints are that drinks are pricey and that they don't let you park your bike out front. Open: sun-thurs 10-1; fri/sat 'til 3. (Map area C7)

De Rokerij - *Singel 8, 422-6643*

This Rokerij is one of the nicest coffeeshops in the Central Station area. There are African-influenced murals on the walls, and low, cushioned seats. Just make sure that you don't sit under one of the spotlights that fade in and out from time to time: unless you're a bit of an exhibitionist, it can be very annoying to be catching a good buzz and suddenly find yourself on centre stage. They also serve alcohol. Check the little blackboard by the entrance to see which nights they're offering freebies like tarot reading or foot massage. (For the record there's another, smaller, Rokerij at Amstel 8, and I've heard that another one is opening soon). Singel branch open: sun-thurs 9-1; fri/sat 'til 2. (Map area D3)

De Overkant - *Van Limburg Stirumplein 20, 686-8957*

Wow - what a great menu. I've never been disappointed by anything I've bought here. Their hash rules! That's why this long-standing, neighbourhood coffeeshop is so popular. There are always several things on special, and if you're looking for something specific, they're patient and give honest advice. The shop itself is small and simply furnished with only a few tables and chairs. In the same neighbourhood you'll find Mind Over Matter (see Smart Shops, Shopping chapter) and Zaal 100 (see Restaurants, Food chapter). Open: sun 12-24; mon-thurs 10-24; fri/sat 10-1. (Map area B2)

De Overkant Hortus - *Nieuwe Herengracht 71, 422-1949*

This recently-renovated Overkant is located right across the canal from the Botanical Gardens (see Museums), close to the Waterlooplein market (see Shopping). It's a small shop, but the simple, uncluttered interior and the big windows make it feel airy and open. They offer the same high quality weed and hash as the original shop, though the selection isn't as large. Smoking a joint here and then exploring the Gardens is a great way to spend an afternoon. Open: daily 10-24. (Map area F6)

Kashmir Lounge - *Jan Pieter Heijestraat 85-87, 683-2268*
http://www.redrival.com/kashmir

This whole place is adorned with Indian metal-work lampshades, embroidered fabrics, and coloured-glass candle holders. One incense-laden room is furnished with patterned carpets, pillows decorated with mirrors, and low wooden tables. It's quite beautiful and the quality of smoke matches the decor. DJs play from time to time and then the place gets pretty packed. In the afternoons it's very mellow. They have a small terrace out front in the summer, too. Open: mon-thurs 10-1; fri/sat 10-3; sun 11-1.

Homegrown Fantasy - *Nieuwezijds Voorburgwal 87a, 627-5683*
http://www.homegrownfantasy.nl

For years, this well-known coffeeshop has had a good reputation for both the quality of their weed and the relaxed atmosphere of the shop. They have a large, tasty selection of Dutch-grown grass and a couple of types of hash. They also serve pots of tea. I like it here best in the daytime when the light is soft and time just seems to slow... right.......down. Be sure to visit the toilet where the black light makes your teeth glow and your pee look like milk! Open: sun-thurs 9-24; fri/sat 'til 1. (Map area D4)

Abraxas - *Jonge Roelensteeg 12-14; 625-5763*
http://www.coffeeshop-abraxas.com

Recent renovations, which include clear glass floors on the upper levels, have breathed new life into this already popular and well-established coffeeshop. The three floors of this old house each have their own style and ambience. Sitting in the uppermost room, for instance, feels like you're visiting an elf's treehouse. And from up there you can also see into the expensive and arty Supperclub across the alley. Several DJs work here, so music tends to be pretty good. It also gets very crowded, especially on weekends. Unfortunately, drinks are way overpriced - bottled juice is *f*4.25 and tea is *f*3.50! Open: daily 10-1. (Map area D5)

Siberië - *Brouwersgracht 11, 623-5909*
http://www.siberie.net

Siberië is a great coffeeshop that caters to an international crowd who appreciate the changing art exhibitions, cool tunes, and of course the smoke. They sell a good variety of dope in all price ranges. And they also have a computer where you can check your email for *f*1. Save time for a walk along the canal where they're located - it's very beautiful. Open: sun-thurs 11-23; fri/sat 11-24. (Map area D3)

de Republiek - *2de Nassaustraat 1a, 682-8431*
http://www.republiek.nl

This cute shop, with connections to Siberië (see above) and Ruigoord (see Festivals, Music chapter), is an institution in this neighbourhood. They've been around for ages, and locals are always dropping by for a smoke and a chat. Upstairs you can check your email. There's also a large assortment of teas including fresh mint and yogi. If you get the munchies, you can buy a piece of fresh fruit for *f*1. Open: daily 11-23. (Map area B2)

A NOTE ABOUT DRUGS IN AMSTERDAM

Once again Holland leads the western world in progressive thinking and action: soft drugs like cannabis and hashish have been decriminalized for over 20 years. Small amounts of these harmless substances can be bought, sold, and consumed without interference by the police.

Trafficking in hard drugs is dealt with seriously, but addiction is considered a matter of health and social well-being rather than a criminal or law enforcement problem. The number of addicts in Holland, where they can receive treatment without fear of criminal prosecution, is much lower than other countries where the law is used to strip people of their human rights (not too mention their property).

Some member states of the European Union (especially France), are putting pressure on Holland to conform to their repressive drug laws. This has resulted in the introduction of new drug policies that, while still more liberal than elsewhere, reflect a regressive trend in the thinking of the Dutch authorities.

The Cannabis College (O.Z. Achterburgwal 124, 423-4420, *http://www.cannabiscollege.com*) is a non-profit organization that was formed in order to educate the public about the cannabis plant and all it's uses. The volunteers who run the college are also dedicated to bringing about an end to the insane and unreasonable punishments inflicted throughout the world on those who choose to use cannabis, for whatever reason. They're located in a 17th century canal house. Stop in to look at the exhibits and see what events are going on. If you want to visit their beautiful garden in the basement, they ask for a donation of *f*5 which is used to help fund the college. In the back is the glass-blowing studio of African Ash, where those awesome glass pipes are created. Open: daily 12-20 (possibly longer in summer; shorter in winter). (Map area D5)

Brandend Zand - *Marnixstraat 92, 528-7292*
http://www.brandendzand.nl

From the big aquarium to the multi-level seating, the interior of this shop is pleasing to the stoned eye. And because it's not right in the centre of town, prices are pretty good, too: both for drinks and smoke. Way in the back there's a pool table. It's near Sagarmatha Seeds (see Seed Shops, below). Open: daily 10-1.

Katsu - *1e Van Der Helststraat 70, 675-2617*

Katsu is a long-standing neighbourhood coffeeshop located just off the Albert Cuyp Market. It's got a shabby, homey feel to it, and some wicked grass. They're famous for their Hazes which give a wonderful cerebral high. Their hash made with the Ice-O-Later (see Pollinator Co, below) is out of this world. Well worth a visit. Open: mon-thurs 11-23; fri/sat 11-24; sun 12-23.

YoYo - *2e Jan v.d. Heydenstraat 79, 664-7173*

YoYo is a perfect place to spend a mellow afternoon reading or writing, while you slowly smoke a joint. The shop is spacious and airy, which is particularly nice if you don't smoke tobacco. As it's a bit out of the centre (near Albert Cuyp Market), you'll find good prices on their organically grown buds. Food and drink are also cheap: cheese tosti - ƒ2; tea - ƒ1.50; organic apple juice - ƒ2. Now if only I could take control of the stereo... Open: mon-sat 12-20 (in winter 'til 19); sun 16-19. (Map E8)

La Tertulia - *Prinsengracht 312*

Plants, flowers and a little fountain give this coffeeshop a tropical feeling, but what I like best about this place is the outdoor terrace they set up in the summer. It's right at the edge of the canal and there are flowers on all the tables. It's easy to find this building: just look for the Van Gogh sunflowers painted all over it. Open: tues-sat 11-19. (Map area C5)

Pi Kunst And Koffie - *2e Laurierdwarsstraat 64, 622-5960*

Pi is an attractive coffeeshop/gallery in the Jordaan with big windows and lots of local art. The main floor has a big bar where you can buy smoke, drinks and snacks. Feel free to use the chess and backgammon boards. In the basement, gamers sit hunched over several computers, smoking joints and killing Orcs. It's a pretty fun place. Open: mon-sat 10-20. (Map area B5)

Paradox - *1e Bloemdwarsstraat 2, 623-5639*
http://www.paradoxamsterdam.demon.nl

Not only can you buy and smoke cannabis here, but the Paradox serves up some delicious food! Their awesome fruit shakes are a bit expensive, but if you've got the dough they're a real treat. A banana/strawberry shake, big enough to share, costs ƒ8.50, and a giant glass of fresh orange juice is ƒ5. Tostis run from ƒ3.50 to ƒ5.50, and they also cook up fresh, home-made soup. Nice decor, and the neighbourhood is beautiful. Open: daily 10-19. (Map area B4)

Dutch Flowers - *Singel 387, 624-7624*
http://www.dutch-flowers.nl

The beautiful canal on one side and an interesting, busy little street on the other make this a nice spot to take a break. There's a stack of magazines and comics, and good music on the stereo. It's located right in the centre of the city by Spui Circle. Their selection of weed and hash is also available in small amounts. *And* they serve beer. Open: sun-thurs 10-1; fri/sat 'til 2. (Map area C6)

Any Time - *Korte Kolksteeg 5, 420-8698*

The first time I walked into this tiny, welcoming coffeeshop, the guy behind the counter offered me a hit from a vaporizer (which they sell here) before I even had my coat off! Now *that's* friendly service. It's not far from Central Station and seems to cater to an international crowd. Across the street there's a brothel with girls in the windows. Oh yeah, and the coffee is terrible - stick to tea or juice. Open: daily 10-1. (Map area D3)

Kadinsky - *Rosmarijnsteeg 9, 624-7023*
http://www.channels.nl/kadinsky.html

A hip coffeeshop with an area upstairs that's perfect for kicking back and smoking that first joint of the day. The music varies from acid jazz to reggae to rock, it just depends on who's working. Delicious cookies are also available. Located on a tiny little street near Spui Circle. Open: daily 10-1. (Map area D5)

Greenhouse Namaste - *Waterlooplein 345, 622-5499*

While the other branches of this coffeeshop seem to have gone downhill in the last couple of years, I still enjoy spending time at this location. It's nice sitting at a candle-lit table, listening to music, smoking a joint, and looking out at City Hall through their big window. And when the weather is good, they have a great terrace out front. Open: sun-thurs 9-1; fri/sat 'til 2. (Map area E6)

The Bluebird - *Sint Antoniesbreestraat 71, 622-5232*
http://www.coffeeshopbluebird.nl

The huge, old menu at the Bluebird was famous for it's variety and the creative way it was displayed. Current laws (see box) have forced them to cut back some on choice, but the quality of their wares remains high. I like to pick something up here and then, if it's sunny, head over to the T-Boat or, if the weather sucks, to the Museum Coffeeshop (see below). Open: daily 9:30-1. (Map area E5)

The T-Boat - *Oude Schans 143*

A coffeeshop on a houseboat. That's pretty cool! I don't buy buds here or hang out inside, but in the summer, on a sunny day, it's fantastic: smoking on the big deck by the water, sipping a juice, getting a tan, watching the ducks and boats cruise by. Located between Nieuwmarkt and Waterlooplein. Open: daily (in summer)10-24. (Map area E5)

Museum Coffeeshop - *Oude Doelenstraat 20, 623-5267*

The owners of the Hash Marijuana Hemp Museum (just a few doors away) have done a nice job fixing up this place. There are lots of hemp decorations and some trippy murals. They don't sell smoke anymore, but you can bring in your own. The corner location and big windows make it a great spot for watching all the sleazy action on the street. Upstairs is a beautiful, North African-style chill-space, but it's not always open so you should ask before you head up. Open: daily 10-1. (Map area E5)

The Otherside - *Reguliersdwarsstraat 6, 421-1014*

As it's located right in the heart of the gay ghetto, it's mostly men that come here, but women are also welcome. It's a friendly spot and it's easy to meet people. The main drawback is the dance music played too loud. Open: daily 11-1. (Map D6)

Tweedy - *Vondelstraat 104, 618-0344*
http://www.tweedy.nl

Tweedy sits at the edge of Vondelpark just across the street from the Vondel Church. I find it a pleasant place to get stoned. I especially like sitting at the back in one of the three train compartments, complete with overhead luggage racks full of magazines and backgammon sets. They also have a pool table, and a good selection of candy bars. Open; daily 10-24 (longer in the summer). (Map area A7)

Marhaba - *Kinkerstraat 12, 777-1171*

The owners of this place splashed out on the decor and have created a very inviting space in which to get ripped. It's a funky, uncrowded place with amicable staff and a pretty nice menu. They play mellow hip-hop and top-40 r&b. Upstairs they have a Dirty Harry pinball (unfortunately the right flipper is a bit fucked). The only problem, other than the broken flipper, is all the west-side dudes hanging here: they're friendly enough, but it would be nice if there were more women in the house. Open: daily 12-1. (Map area B6)

De Kuil - *Oudebrugsteeg 27, 623-4848*

A slightly older crowd hangs here because of the classic rock on the sound-system. This area around the Damrak is pretty sleazy, but the shop itself is clean, comfortable, and very tourist friendly. They have a good selection of smoke on offer and it's one of those places where it's always 4:20. They also serve alcohol, though they advise you not to mix the two. Open: sun-thurs 10-1; fri/sat 10-3. (Map area D4)

SEEDS / GROW SHOPS

There are several reputable places to buy seeds around town, but over the past couple of years a lot of fly-by-night companies have also appeared selling inferior products. The reputable companies have spent years developing their strains in order to produce a stable, reliable seed. I've listed a few of them below. Remember that while it's legal to buy cannabis seeds in the Netherlands, it's illegal to import them into most other countries. You've been warned.

Sagarmatha Seeds and Psychedelic Gallery - *Marnixstraat 255, 638-4334*
http://www.highestseeds.com

This company's motto, "highest on earth", refers in part to their name. Sagarmatha is what they call Mount Everest in Nepal. The 100% organically produced seeds sold here aren't super cheap, but they're aimed at connoisseurs, who will appreciate the end result. They sell some very tasty strains including Bubbleberry, Mangolian Indica, and the particularly pleasurable Matanuska Tundra (a.k.a. Alaskan Thunderfuck). Check their web site for news, images of resin-coated plants, and some interesting links (see also 'Shrooms, Shopping chapter). Open: mon-sat 12-17. (Map area B4)

Sensi Seeds - *Oudezijds Achterburgwal 150, 624-0386*
http://www.sensiseeds.com
The people who brought you the Hash Marijuana Hemp Museum run this business, too. You'll find everything you need for growing on sale here, starting with seeds. Like Sagarmatha, the seed prices are a bit high, but they have proven genetic quality and that attracts a lot of professional growers. They're always big winners at the Cannabis Cup awards (see Festivals, Music chapter). It's worth stopping in here just to pick up their colour catalogue full of photos of beautiful buds. They also have a small shop near Central Station, at Nieuwendijk 26. Open: mon-sat 11-21; sun 11-18. (Map area E5)

Pollinator Company - *Cornelis Trooststraat 37, 470-8889*
http://www.pollinator.nl
This inviting shop caters to all your post-harvest needs. They invented and sell the amazing Pollinator (for making hash), seed sorters, and even a machine called The Clipper that automatically manicures your buds! Their newest development is the incredible Ice-o-lator. It's un-fucking-believable how good the hash is that's made from this simple machine. This is definitely the only store of its kind that I've ever heard of. It's also the home of the Botanic Herbalist (see 'Shrooms, Shopping chapter), and a couple of doors down is a grow shop called Positive Grow. After The Harvest is open: mon-sat 11-19.

Emerald Triangle Seed Company - *Prins Hendrikkade 87, 777-2767*
Amsterdam's newest seed company is also it's oldest, selling original Seed Bank stock. Over many years these strains have earned the respect of growers the world over. Stop by the "Home of the Haze" and check it out. Open: daily 10-18 (though you may have to knock loudly to get in as the owner tends to snooze for awhile in the afternoon). (Map area E4)

T.H.Seeds - *Nieuwendijk 13, 421-1762*
http://www.thseeds.com
Hemp Works (see below) sell their own, in-house line - T.H.Seeds. Strains available include the incredible S.A.G.E., Chocolate Chunk, and their newest variety, The Hog. Make your purchase during their 4:20 happy hour and get 10% off. That's also when you're most likely to find their resident seed expert, Adam, in the house. He knows a fuck of a lot about growing and is happy to share his knowledge. Open: daily 12-19. (Map area D3)

The Flying Dutchman - *Oudezijds Achterburgwal 131, 428-4023*
http://www.flyingdutchmen.com
This company sells their seeds from their pleasant shop of the same name, which is located in the Red Light District, just across the canal from the Cannabis College (see below). Choose from their own line, or from one of the other companies' products that are also available here. And take some time to look over their impressive selection òf glass pipes. Open: daily 11-19. (Map area E5)

Paradise Seeds - *679-5422*
http://www.paradise-seeds.com
I don't know too much about this company, but I had the pleasure recently of smoking some hash that originated from one of their seeds and it was delicious. Call to find out where they're available.

Interpolm Amsterdam - *Prins Hendrikkade 11, 627-7750*
http://www.interpolm.nl

These guys are very conveniently located just across from Central Station. In addition to the grow equipment showroom, there's a little café, too. Open: mon 13-18; tues-fri 10-18; sat 10-17. (Map area E3)

De Groeiwinkel - *Javastraat 74, 663-6378*

New and used growing supplies are sold here, as are seeds and a particularly nice soil mix. If you make the trek out east where this shop is located, think about visiting the Ij Brewery, the Troppenmuseum, and the Dapper Market as they're all in the same area (see the relevant chapters for details). Open: mon-sat 11-19. (Map area F7)

Seeds of Passion - *Utrechtsestraat 26, 625-1100*
http://www.greenlands.nl

The interesting thing about this seed outlet is that they sell strains developed in countries other than Holland. (Map area E7)

HEMP STORES

Hemp Works - *Nieuwendijk 13, 421-1762*
http://www.xs4all.nl/~hemp

"Industrial Organic Wear". This is a designer hemp store. Most of what they carry, like the 100% hemp baseball shirts, are on their own label. Other hemp clothes include jeans, dresses and lingerie, all displayed against a backdrop of hemp walls! They also sell hand-blown glass pipes. At the lounge in the back of the shop, DJs spin hip-hop and drum & bass. If you like those sounds, check out the monthly drum & bass parties they organize at Club More (see Clubs, Music chapter). Open: daily 12-19. (Map area D3)

Sensi Seeds Hemp Store - *Oudezijds Achterburgwal 148, 624-0386*

The owners have some exciting plans for a broad-range hemp store at this address, with unique products produced right here in the Netherlands as well as others from around the world. It's still in the planning stages, but hopefully it'll be open by the time you get here.

SHOPPING

Saturdays, at 17 or 18:00, most stores in Amsterdam lock their doors and they don't open again until Monday afternoon. However, many stores in "tourist areas" are now allowed to open on Sunday. Most stores stay open on Thursdays 'til 21:00.

MARKETS

Albert Cuyp Markt - *Albert Cuypstraat (btwn Ferdinand Bolstr. & Van Woustr.)*
http://www.albertcuypmarkt.com

It's big and it's great! Amsterdam's most famous market is crowded with stalls and shoppers. You'll find everything here, from fruits and veggies, to clothes and hardware. Underwear is a good deal and so are plain cotton t-shirts (if yours are getting smelly). Just remember that you don't pick your own fruit and some of the vendors are assholes and will routinely slip a few rotten pieces into each bag. This happens to tourists and Dutch shoppers alike, so don't take it personally and don't be afraid to complain. To pick your own produce, shop at the Turkish stores that are found around most markets. Open: mon-sat 9-16. (Map area E8)

Organic Farmers' Market - *Noordermarkt*

Its location at the foot of the Noorderkerk (North Church) lends a medieval feel to this fantastic organic market. All the booths sell healthy produce and products. Consequently, it's not really cheap, but if you like markets it's well worth a visit. Right around the corner, on the same day, is the Lindengracht market (see below). Another organic market (that also takes place on Saturdays) can be found at Nieuwmarkt from 9 to 16:00. The Noordermarkt is open Saturdays from 9 to 16:00, too. (Map C3)

Lindenmarkt - *Lindengracht*

This is an all-purpose market that's a bit more expensive than Albert Cuyp, but still has some good deals. It's in a beautiful neighbourhood and is right around the corner from the Organic Farmers' Market (see above). Open: sat 9-15. (Map area C3)

Noordermarkt - *Noordermarkt*

For all you die-hard shoppers with nowhere else to go on Monday morning, this market's for you. There's both used and new clothes, books, records, and all kinds of junk. Great for bargain hunting. After it closes you can often find good stuff in the garbage. And just for the record, there have been markets at this location since 1627! Open: mon 9-12. (Map area C3)

Dappermarkt - *Dapperstraat*

A lot of immigrants from North Africa and the Middle East shop at this all-purpose market, which is the cheapest in Amsterdam. There's also an Egyptian guy there who sells tasty falafels for ƒ6. It's close to Oosterpark (see Parks, Hanging Out chapter), and the windmill (see Ij Brewery, Bars chapter). Open: mon-sat 9-16. (Map area H7)

Ten Kate Market - *Ten Katestraat*

It's a bit out of the way for most tourists, but if you're in the area pay a visit to this lively neighbourhood market. I go there regularly to buy cheap popcorn from the

Turkish shops. Kinkerstraat, the main shopping street running by Ten Katestraat, lacks charm, but the streets behind the market are pretty. Open: mon-sat 9-17. (Map A6)

Waterlooplein Market - *Waterlooplein*

This square is home to a terrific flea market where you can find clothes and jewellery and junk. It's easy to spend a couple of hours wandering around and, unlike other Amsterdam markets, you can try bargaining. Open: mon-sat 10-17. (Map E6)

De Rommelmarkt - *Looiersgracht 38*

From the entrance, this flea market appears to be just a small storefront, but if you go in you'll find a sprawling 2 floors of old stuff. It's a lot of fun even if it's not the cheapest of markets. Mondays - mostly stamps, coins and cards. Tuesdays - mostly books, records, etc. Wednesdays - everything. Thursdays - second hand clothes. Fridays - closed. Saturdays - everything. Sundays - antiques. Open: 11-17. (Map B6)

Flower Market - *Singel*

This pretty market is full of flowers and plants that are sold from barges on the Singel canal between Koningsplein and Muntplein. There are lots of good deals and it's probably the best place to buy tulip bulbs. Even if you're not interested in shopping here, it's a pretty market to wander through. (Map area D6)

BOOKS, MAGAZINES & COMICS

Kok Antiquariaat - *Oude Hoogstraat 14-18, 623-1191*

This is one of the best used bookstores in Amsterdam. It's spacious and well organized, with a lot of English titles. English literature is upstairs. Open: mon-fri 9:30-18; sat 9:30-17. (Map area D5)

The American Book Center - *Kalverstraat 185, 625-5537*
http://www.abc.nl

I think this is the cheapest store for new books, especially for students, who get a 10% discount. They are the largest source of English-language books in Europe! Look for bargains in the basement. A few times a year they clear out all the old magazines and you can sometimes find some good stuff for about ƒ2.50. And if you're here on the American Thanksgiving, everything is discounted an additional 10%! The Kalverstraat is one of the main car-free shopping streets in the city. Open: mon-sat 10-20 (thurs 'til 22); sun 11-19. (Map area D5)

Barry's Book Exchange - *Kloveniersburgwal 58, 626-6266*

Everything is very well organized in this clean shop (there's none of that mustiness associated with so many used book stores) and you're bound to find something of interest. They have a big travel section with both guides and literature, and there's a German and French section, too. If you have some books to sell, I find that they pay the fairest price in town. Open: mon-fri 10:30-18; sat 10:30-17:30; sun 11:30-16. (Map area E5)

J. de Slegte Boekhandel - *Kalverstraat 48-52, 622-5933*

Some good deals on remainders can be found at this big store on the Kalverstraat. It lacks the charm of KOK (see above), but upstairs you'll find a huge selection of used books, many in English (I recently found a rare Philip K. Dick novel for ƒ10). Open: mon 11-18; tues-fri 9:30-18 (thurs 'til 21); sat 9:30-18; sun 12-17. (Map area D5)

Vrouwen in Druk - *Westermarkt 5, 624-5003*

A small, women's bookstore across from the beautiful, old Westerkerk and the Homomonument. Mostly used books as well as magazines and postcards. Open: mon-fri 11-18; sat 11-17. (Map area C4)

Vrolijk - *Paleisstraat 135, 623-5142*
http://www.xs4all.nl/~vrolijk

This shop advertises itself as "the largest gay and lesbian bookstore on the continent". It's located just off the Dam Square and it's usually pretty busy. If you're looking for something in particular, the staff are friendly and helpful. Open: mon 11-18; tues-fri 10-18 (thurs 'til 21); sat 10-17. (Map area D5)

Intermale - *Spuistraat 251, 625 0009*
http://www.intermale.nl

This is a gay bookstore. It's a nice space with a good selection of books, magazines and some videos. They have gay guides to countries all around the world and a small porno section in the back. Open: mon 11-18; tues-sat 10-18; (thurs 'til 21). (Map area C5)

Vandal Com-x - *Rozengracht 31, 420-2144*
http://www.vandalcomx.com

Definitely check this place out if you're into action figures: they've got them from floor to ceiling. It's where I got my much admired "Radioactive Cornholio". They also sell trading cards, shirts, and more. The comix are at their other shop a few doors down the street. Open: tues-fri 11-18; sat 11-17; sun 12-17. (Map area B5)

Henk Lee's Comics & Manga Store - *Zeedijk 136, 421-3688*
http://www.comics.nl

Located in Amsterdam's tiny Chinatown, Henk's store is stuffed full of comics, toys, and trading cards. His specialty is manga, so check here if you're into that. Other shops to check for manga are Profesor Ich (Koninginneweg 218, 675-5663), or the bookshop in the basement of the Hotel Okura (Ferdinand Bolstraat 333, 679-9238). Henk Lee open: mon-sat 11-18 (thurs 'til 21); sun 12-18. (Map area E4)

Gallerie Lambiek - *Kerkstraat 78, 626-7543*
http://www.lambiek.net

This is the most famous comic store in Amsterdam. They've got new, used and fanzines too. It's interesting to look over all the European comics, but it ain't cheap. Open: mon-fri 11-18; sat 11-17; sun 13-17. (Map area C7)

Evenaar - *Singel 348, 624-6289*

This travel bookshop has a fascinating collection. Works are organized by region and include not only guides and journals, but novels, political analyses and history - many by lesser known authors. Worth visiting for a browse if you're travelling onward from Holland. Open: mon-fri 12-18; sat 11-17. (Map area C5)

Athenaeum Nieuwscentrum - *Spui 14-16, 624-2972*
http://www.athenaeum.nl

For cheap magazines, check the bargain bin at this news shop on Spui Circle. I buy old *NME*'s here for ƒ.50 and other music mags in the ƒ1 to ƒ4 range. For new magazines and international papers, this is one of the best stores in Amsterdam. The sister bookstore next door is excellent, but not cheap. Open: mon-sat 8-21; sun 10-18. (Map area D5)

Van Gennep - *Nieuwezijds Voorburgwal 330, 626-4448*

This is a "remainder" bookstore with an impressive collection of quality English books, and prices start as low as ƒ5. Great for bargain hunting. Near Spui Circle. Open: mon 11-18; tues-fri 10-18 (thurs 'til 21:00); sat 11-18. (Map area D5)

Book Traffic - *Leliegracht 50, 620-4690*

The owner of this used bookshop's got lots of English books and, sometimes, a bargain bin out front. There are a few other used bookshops located on this beautiful canal, too. Open: mon-fri 10-18; sat 11-18; sun 13-18. (Map area C4)

Het Fort Van Sjakoo - *Jodenbreestraat 24, 625-8979*
http://www.xs4all.nl/~sjakoo

"Specializes in Libertarian and radical ideas from the first to the fifth world and beyond". In addition to political books from around the world, this volunteer-run shop has a whole wall of fanzines and magazines, including lots of info on squatting. They've got music, cards, stickers, and shirts, too. Definitely worth a visit. The basement is home to the ASCII internet café (see Hanging Out chapter). Open: mon-fri 11-18; sat 11-17. (Map area E6)

Cultural - *Gasthuismolensteeg 4*

This hole-in-the wall bookstore has a few shelves of English paperbacks and a few piles of *Life* and other magazines from the '50s and '60s. It's not far from Dam square in a pretty area, so you might pass it while wandering about, but I forgot to check the opening hours. Sorry. (Map area C5)

Oudemanhuis Boekenmarkt - *Oudemanhuispoort*

This little book market is located in the neighbourhood of the university, in a covered alleyway that runs between Oudezijds Achterburgwal and Kloveniersburgwal. Used books and magazines in several languages are spread out on tables and stands. There are also maps, cards and, occasionally, funny pornographic etchings from centuries past for ƒ1 to ƒ2. In the middle there's an entrance to a pretty courtyard with benches where you can rest your legs. Open: mon-sat 10-16. (Map area E5)

RECORDS & CDs

Boudisque - *Haringpakkerssteeg 10-18, 623-2603*
http://www.boudisque.nl

This is one of Amsterdam's best music stores. They have a big selection and they know what's hot. Lots of pop, punk, metal and dance, as well as music from all around the world. Mostly CDs, but still some vinyl. Open: mon 12-18; tues-sat 10-18 (thurs 'til 21); sun 12-18. (Map area E3)

Roots - *Jonge Roelensteeg 6, 620-4470*

Reggae lovers take note: the hole-in-the-wall in the alley that houses this shop is full of Jamaican beats - from roots to dancehall and beyond. Check the African section, too. They stock some vinyl, but most of their collection consists of CDs, including a lot of re-issues at very affordable prices. The owners are a great source of information about festivals in and around Amsterdam. Open: tues-sat 10:30-18 (thurs 'til 21); sun/mon 12:30-18. (Map area D5)

Concerto - *Utrechtsestraat 54-60, 624-5467*
http://www.netcetera.nl/jazzfacts/concerto

New and used records, tapes and CDs in a pretty neighbourhood. Good prices on used stuff and lots of vinyl. Well worth checking out. Open: mon-sat 10-18 (thurs 'til 21); sun 12-18. (Map area E7)

Get Records - *Utrechtsestraat 105, 622-3441*

While they mostly carry CDs here, there's still some vinyl that's worth digging into. They have a very select, up-to-date collection of pop, indie, funk, etc. Open: mon 12-18; tues-sat 10-18 (thurs 'til 21); sun 12-18. (Map area E7)

Fat Beats - *Singel 10 (basement), 423-0886*
http://www.fatbeats.com

Fat Beats is the store to check out if you're looking for the newest hip-hop on vinyl. Much of it is independent and underground - there's a lot of white label stuff here. You'll also find some r&b and funk. DJs often hang out and spin a few tracks in the basement. Also for sale is a small selection of CDs, tapes, and clothing. Open: mon-sat 12-19 (thurs 'til 21); sun 12-18. (Map area D3)

Staalplaat - *Staalkade 6, 625-4176*
http://www.staalplaat.com

You'll find this store appropriately located in a stark, concrete basement not far from the Waterlooplein flea market (see Markets, this chapter). It stocks a huge selection of underground music: industrial, experimental, electronic, noise. They fill mail orders world-wide. This is also a good place to look for flyers advertising live performances of experimental music. Open: mon-fri 11-18; sat 11-17. (Map area E6)

Back Beat Records - *Egelantiersstraat 19, 627-1657*

Jazz, soul, funk, pop, blues, r&b: there's a lot packed into this store's three levels. It's not cheap, but what a selection. It's located in the Jordaan. Open: mon-fri 11-18; sat 10-17. (Map area C4)

Record Palace - *Weteringschans 33, 622-3904*

This is another good place for collectors: they have sections for most kinds of music. Check out the autographed record covers on the wall. It's located across the street from the famous Paradiso (see Music chapter). Open: mon-fri 11-18; sat 11-17; sun 12-17. (Map area C7)

Distortion Records - *Westerstraat 72, 627-0004, http://www.xs4all.nl/~distort*

They advertise "loads of noise, lo-fi, punk rock, and indie". Collectors, especially of vinyl, are going to love this place. The owners here are definitely on top of things, and they have a good selection of dance music now, too. They're located just up the street from the Noorderkerk (see Markets, this chapter). Open: tues-fri 11-18 (thurs 'til 21); sat 10-18. (Map area C3)

Record Mania - *Hazenstraat 29, 620-9912*

Vinyl rules at this little shop in the Jordaan. It's beautiful to see all the bins full of LPs and singles just waiting to be browsed through. They also have some *f*1 and *f*2.50 bins. Open: tues-sat 13-18. (Map area B5)

De Plaatboef - *Rozengracht 40, 422-8777*

"The Record Thief" has several stores around Holland. The Amsterdam store is very popular. They sell new and used CDs and LPs. My friend scored a really hot Fela Kuti record here for cheap. There's also a small box in the back which occasionally has old issues of *Mojo* and other magazines for *f*2-5. Open: mon 12-18; tues-sat 10-18 (thurs 'til 21). (Map area B4)

Groove Connection - *St. Nicolaasstraat 41, 624-7234*

Apparently, this is a really popular place with DJs, who come to hear what's new and hot. I like it because it makes me feel stoned when I step inside. If you're into cool dance music (in other words, stuff that ain't shit), you should drop by. (You might also want to check Outland Records at Zeedijk 22.) Open: mon 14-18; tues-sat 11-18 (thurs 'til 21); sun 14-18. (Map area D4)

Sound of the Fifties - *Prinsengracht 669, 623-9745*

Funk, soul, jazz, r&b, gospel and more. Prices aren't super cheap, but there are some gems to be found here. New and used. Open: mon 13-18; tues-sat 11:30-18. (Map area C6)

Nauta - *Singel 87, 625-2345*

I wandered into this unassuming shop and found some great records. They don't have too much stock on hand, but cool stuff keeps popping up. Check the books and magazines, too. Open: mon, wed, fri 12-18; sat 12-17. (Map area D4)

Wentelwereld - *1e Bloemdwarsstraat 13a, 622-2330*

I was riding through the Jordaan and my eye spotted the row of *f*2,50 bins at this used record store. I came out with a copy of *The Runaways Live in Japan*. Open: tues-sat 12-17:30. (Map area B4)

Datzzit - *Prinsengracht 306, 622-1195*

This record store is full of collectables. And not just records. They also have books, posters, some old toys, and other stuff. Open: mon-sat 10-18; sun 12-18. (Map C5)

Forever Changes - *Bilderdijkstraat 148, 612-6378*

This is a well-stocked store full of new and used records and CDs. They have really interesting stuff in many areas: '60s, punk, blues... and check out the singles boxes on the counter. There are also some fanzines. Open: mon 13-18; tues-fri 10-18; sat 10-17. (Map area A6)

Independent Outlet - *Vijzelstraat 77, 421-2096*
http://www.outlet.nl

Punk and hardcore central. Vinyl (of course), and CDs. (see Misc, this chapter). Open: tues-fri 11-19 (thurs 'til 21); sat 11-18; sun 13-18. (Map area D7)

CLUB FASHIONS

Amsterdam's club fashion shops stock a wide variety of designer labels, both international and local. They're also all good places to find information on parties and raves.

Clubwear-House - *Herengracht 265, 622-8766*
http://www.clubwearhouse.nl

Come inside where it's always friendly and always trippy. You can listen to young DJs (who are encouraged to come by and show off their stuff) while you check out wild clothing by new designers on their in-house label, CWH. Tickets and flyers for all the best parties are available here, too. They have a sister store, Cyberdog, at Spuistraat 250. Clubwear-House open: mon-fri 13-18; tues-fri 11-18 (thurs 'til 20:30); sat 12-18. (Map area C5)

Housewives and Haircuts on Fire - *Spuistraat 102, 422-1067*
http://www.xs4all.nl/~housew

If you want to prepare a bit before you hit Amsterdam's clubs, stop into this multidimensional shop. Browse through the club and loungewear for something new. Then have one of the hairdressers do something funky to your head. They also do henna tattoos and glitter body art. It's a pretty chill place and it's right in the centre of town. Open: mon-sat 11-19 (thurs 'til 22). (Map area D4)

Diablo - *Oudezijds Voorburgwal 242, 623-4506*

Lots of intriguing clothing and accessories await you in this dark, grungy store. You should be able to find something new and different here, and at pretty reasonable prices. Open: mon-fri 11-18; sat 10-18. (Map area D5)

Webers Holland - *Kloveniersburgwal 26, 638-1777*

It's not cheap, but the interesting, avant-garde fashions in this store are by Dutch designers. And it's kind of weird. Open: mon 13-19; tues-sat 11-19. (Map area E5)

BODY ART

Elektra - *Eerste Anjeliersdwarsstraat 16, 777-3863*
http://www.elektratattoo.com

Check this out - a tattoo shop owned and operated by women. It's very relaxing here and the good vibes, custom art-work and changing exhibitions offer a refreshing alternative to the heavily male atmosphere of so many tattoo parlours. Open: wed-sun 13-19. (Map area C3)

Body Manipulations - *Oude Hoogstraat 31, 420-8085*
http://www.channels.nl/bodyman.html

Along with tattoos, piercing is probably the most popular form of body art. They used to offer scarification and branding here, but now it's just piercing. The people who run the studio are more than happy to talk to you about the procedure and what pain (if any), is involved. They also have an excellent collection of books and magazines on the subject. Prices start at ƒ15 for an ear piercing (including stud), and ƒ30 for cartilage. Lip or eyebrow costs ƒ50. And tongue, nipple, navel, clit, penis, etc, start at ƒ50 (excluding jewellery). Open: mon-wed 12-18; thurs-sat 12-19. (Map area E5)

Hair Police - Kerkstraat 113, 420-5841

While they do regular cuts, too, this place was one of the first in town to do wild styles. They're responsible for popularizing dreads, extensions and colours in Amsterdam, and an appointment is recommended. The ground floor, under Hair Police, is occupied by the beautiful tattoo shop, Eyegasm. Open: tues-fri 12-19 (thurs 'til 20); sat 12-18. (Map area C7)

Purple Circle - *Geelvinckssteeg 10, 620-7662*
http://www.purple-circle.com

There's a Purple Circle in LA and now there's one here, too. The scissor-happy stylists at this cool studio operate out of a hole-in-the-wall near the Flower Market. They also specialize in dreads, braids, extensions, and colours. Open: tues-sat 12-19. (Map area D6)

CHOCOLATE

Bon Bon Jeanette - *Central Station 421-5194*

So fucking good! Jeanette's amazing chocolates are all made with organic ingredients. *And* they contain a third less sugar than most other chocolates. Open: mon-sat 8-21; sun 10-20

Australian Homemade - *Leidsestraat 59, 622-0897; Singel 437, 428-7533*
http://www.australianhomemade.com

This company uses only natural ingredients (no preservatives, dyes, or artificial colouring) to produce some damn good ice-cream, milkshakes, and delicious chocolates. I usually pick-up a pre-packaged "bar", that contains 5 assorted chocolates, for ƒ4,95. They're decorated with gold-leaf and are almost too pretty to eat. Open: sun/mon 12-18; tues-sat 10:30-18 (thurs 'til 21). (Map area C6)

Leonidas Bon Bons - *Damstraat 15, 625-3497; Schiphol Airport 653-5077*
http://www.leonidas.com

The Belgians know what they're doing when it comes to chocolate, even when they're a big company like this one. Their small (250 gram, ƒ10) box of assorted chocolates makes a nice gift, and the price at the airport branch is the same as in the city. Grab some for yourself, too, and you won't have to eat that crappy airplane food! Damstraat branch open: mon-sat 9-18 (thurs 'til 21); sun 11-18. Schiphol open: daily 7-22. (Map area D5)

SMART SHOPS & 'SHROOM VENDORS

Surprise! You can buy magic mushrooms over the counter at several shops around town. Since the Dutch Ministry of Health has not found them to be hazardous when used responsibly, the government has decided to tolerate the sale of these little buggers in an open (hence, safe) manner. If you haven't tripped before make sure to consult with the person who's selling them first. They'll tell you how to take them and what to expect.

Obviously, if mushrooms and spores are illegal where you're from (and they probably are) then I'm not recommending that you buy them for export.

'Shrooms are also sold at "smart shops". These shops specialize in legal, mostly herbal, mind- and mood-enhancers of various sorts: stimulants, aphrodisiacs, relaxants, and hallucinogens. Smart shops have sprung up all around town over the last few years. Here are a few of the more established and reputable ones.

Kokopelli - *Warmoesstraat 12, 421-7000*
http://www.consciousdreams.nl/shops/amsterdam/kokopelli

Opened by the Conscious Dreams crew (see below), this is one of the hippest smart shops in Amsterdam. The space is beautiful - with a very mellow area at the back where you can drink a tea, surf the Net, listen to DJs, and enjoy the beautiful view over the water. The staff are tourist-friendly, so feel free to ask for info on herbal ecstasy, mushrooms, smart drugs, or any of the other products on offer. There's talk of turning the basement into a living-room-like chill space for meditation and Ayahuasca sessions. It's located very close to Central Station. Open: daily 11-22. (Map area E4)

Conscious Dreams - *Kerkstraat 117, 626-6907*
http://www.consciousdreams.nl

This was the first smart shop in the world! They pioneered the concept and it's always worth dropping into this shop/internet gallery to see what's new. They have a good selection of smart drugs and they're happy to advise and inform you about their different uses. There's also organic cola and lemonade, and coffee or tea are only ƒ1.50 a cup. You can get online (ƒ1 for 5 minutes; ƒ10 an hour) or do some gaming at one of several high-speed computer terminals. You'll also find lots of flyers for parties. It's a very trippy place. Come in... and be experienced. Open: daily 11-19. (Map area C7)

Mind Over Matter - *Van Stirumplein 24, 681-7087*
http://go.to/mindovermatter

Another member of the Conscious Dreams family, this homey shop is filled with new-age stuff, an assortment of smart products - like herbal ecstacy and aphrodisiacs - and small, hand-made gifts. It's also a production office for local dance parties, so check out the flyers for cool gigs. The Overkant (see Coffeeshops, Cannabis chapter) is right next door. Open: mon-thurs 12-21; fri/sat 12-22. (Map area B2)

The Botanic Herbalist - *Cornelis Trooststraat 37, 470-0889,*
http://www.pollinator.nl/Botanic-Herbalist.htm

A very cool store. This space, which they share with the Pollinator Company (see Grow Shops, Cannabis chapter) is a centre for people interested in psychoactive plants. Many are for sale, like the rare Salvia, and the staff at this laid-back shop know all about them and their uses. There are a few hemp products for sale in addition to mushrooms and - get this - mushroom growing equipment! Open: mon-sat 11-19:00.

The Headshop - *Kloveniersburgwal 39, 624-9061*
http://www.headshop.nl

Mushrooms and spores are sold at competitive prices at this cool shop. It's conveniently located in the centre (see Misc, below). Open: mon-sat 11-18. (Map area E5)

Sagarmatha Seeds and Psychedelic Gallery - *Marnixstraat 255, 638-4334*
http://www.highestseeds.com

This shop, located in a cosy old storefront (see Seeds, Cannabis chapter), stocks the widest variety of mushrooms in Amsterdam. And the most potent, too. They were the first in town to sell the fabled Philosophers' Stones. Stop in for experienced advice. Open: mon-sat 12-17. (Map area B4)

Mushroom Galaxy - *Halvemaansteeg 12*
http://www.mushroomgalaxy.com

This tourist-friendly store focuses on natural products: herbs, extracts, teas, peyote, and cannabis seeds. They also carry jewellery, pipes, other gift items, and a new book they publish themselves called *The Ultimate Coffeeshop Guide*. Open: mon-sat 11-23; sun 12-23 (with shorter hours in winter). (Map area D6)

MISCELLANEOUS

The Headshop - *Kloveniersburgwal 39, 624-9061*
http://www.headshop.nl

Most, if not all, your drug paraphernalia needs can be met in the shops on the streets heading east off Dam square past the Grand Hotel Krasnapolsky (which, by the way, has very nice, clean toilets upstairs to the left off the lobby). I think the best store is The Headshop, which has been in business since 1968. Lots and lots of pipes, bongs and papers; plus books, magazines, postcards, stickers and the required collection of incense and Indian clothing. They also sell magic mushrooms and spores for growing your own. They have a good reputation and sometimes it gets very crowded. The Headshop is open: mon-sat 11-18. (Map area E5)

Independent Outlet - *Vijzelstraat 77, 421-2096*
http://www.outlet.nl

IO is a way cool store selling punk and hardcore records, skateboards, clothing, hard-to-find fanzines and magazines, funky lunchboxes, and more. And the stylin' clothes on offer are pretty cheap for Northern Europe. This is also a good place to find out about skate events and where punk and hardcore bands are playing. If you're lucky, you might be here when they have one of their in-store shows: ask at the counter. Open: tues-fri 11-19 (thurs 'til 21); sat 11-18; sun 13-18. (Map area D7)

Open - *Nieuwezijds Voorburgwal 291, 528-6963*
www.openshopamsterdam.com

What a great idea: a funky gift shop with inexpensive stuff that's open when other shops are closed. The owner has an eye for fun, funny, and useful items that make unusual gifts. She sells cute clothing, make-up, toys, and bric-a-brac starting at *f*1,50. And the stock is always changing - look out for CDs and videos, too. Open: tues-sun 4-11 (or whenever the sign outside is lit up). (Map area C5)

African Ash - *various locations*

If you're a pot smoker then you already know that glass pipes are the way to go. The artisans at African Ash do beautiful work, whether they're making a simple pocket pipe, or an incredible dragon that wouldn't be out of place in a museum. You can buy their glass at several places around town including the Flying Dutchman, Kashmir Lounge, and Barney's (see Cannabis chapter). Stop by their workshop which is appropriately situated in the back of the Cannabis College (see Cannabis chapter), and you might get to see them in action.

Aboriginal Art and Instruments - *Paleisstraat 137, 423-1333*
http://www.aboriginalart.nl

This is the only store of it's kind in Europe, so it's no surprise that I'd never seen such beautiful didgeridoos until I wandered into this shop/gallery. The owner travels to the outback in Australia and hand-picks these unique instruments himself to make sure that he gets only the highest quality. Also for sale are CDs and other Aboriginal artwork. If you already have a didgeridoo, stop by for info about jam sessions. Open: tues-sat 12-18; sun 14-18. (Map area D5)

Shamanismo Botanica - *Hemonystraat 51, 673-4682*

The vibe is so relaxed and unassuming in this shop that I almost felt like I was visiting a friend's apartment. The interesting and varied items for sale here include an impressive selection of herbs and "ethno-botanical" plants from around the world, music and musical instruments, and new-agey stuff. If none of that interests you, plop down in the back and try one of the fresh, organic juices - they're cheap and delicious. On Thursday nights at 19:00 they serve up a healthy, veggie meal for only *f*12.50. It's best to call first and reserve. After dinner everyone hangs out, drinking chai and making music. Shop open: tues-sat 11:30-18.

Humana - *Gravenstraat 22, 623-3214*

If you like shopping for used clothes, stop by this store. It's really hit and miss. Sometimes they have only shit, but I've also found some fantastic deals on all kinds of stuff: perfect Levis for ƒ18, a leather jacket for ƒ35, and once they had a big rummage sale and I bought a TV for ƒ12! The money goes to third world development projects. They also accept donations, if you want to lighten your pack a bit. Open: mon 13-18; tues-fri 9:30-18 (thurs 'til 21); sat 9:30-17; sun 12-17. (Map area D4)

The Fair Trade Shop - *Heiligeweg 45, 625-2245*

Crafts, clothes and jewelry from developing countries. Also: fair-trade coffee, tea, chocolate, nuts and wine. Lots of unusual gift ideas. It's not the cheapest store, but there are some deals, and the money is going back to the right people. Open: mon 13-18; tues-fri 10-18 (thurs 'til 21), sat 10-17:30; sun 12-17. (Map area D6)

The Emerald Triangle Trading Company - *Prins Hendrikkade 87, 777-2767*

Located in an old house right across the street from Central Station, this tiny store sells shirts, some glass pipes (pick up a small one to use while you're here), and a few books and other gifts items. This is also the home of the Emerald Triangle Seed Bank (see Seed/Grow Shops, Cannabis chapter). And they sell mushrooms. Open: daily 10-21 (shorter hours in winter). (Map area E3)

The Old Man - *Damstraat 16, 627-0043*

This is a drug paraphernalia shop with a wide choice of pipes. Up one set of stairs you'll come upon a baffling array of weapons and lots of posters of chicks with guns. Some of you might be more comfortable up the other stairs where they sell snowboards, skateboards, and inline skates. Open: mon 10-18; tues-sat 9:30-18 (thurs/fri 'til 21); sun 10:30-18. Hours are sometimes extended in summer. (Map area D5)

China Town Liquor Store - *Geldersekade 94-96, 624-5229*

For some reason I think that this liquor store is cheaper than others, but I don't know if it's true. Anyway, this sleazy strip is where I buy my booze and a couple of doors down is a great Chinese supermarket, Wah Nam Hong. There's a swankier liquor store in the basement of the Albert Heijn on Nieuwezijds Voorburgwal (see Supermarkets, Food chapter) that's open longer hours. The China Town Liquor Store is open: mon-sat 9-18. (Map area E4)

Cash Converters - *Amstelveenseweg 39, 685-0500*

If you like collecting junk, swing by this second-hand store at the far end of Vondelpark. Some things are ridiculously overpriced, but other stuff is a steal. I bought a really nice turntable here for next to nothing. And I got a hot-air popcorn popper. My friend found a Funkadelic CD for ƒ10. Anyway, don't go out of your way, but if you decide to sell your walkman or you're looking for something specific, it could be worth a visit. You can bargain here, too. Open: mon 13-18; tues-fri 10-18 (thurs 'til 21); sat 10-17.

Sil-Screen - *Plantage Doklaan 8-12*

Walk in the front door of this big squatted building and all the way down the long hall to the back. That's where you'll find this little shop selling "crazy" silk-screened clothing by a local artist. Her designs are printed on everything from shirts to underwear. There's also jewellery, cards, and a few other things scattered about, and the prices are low. Make sure you stop at the awesome bakery on your way out (see Bread, Food chapter). Open: only on wed, 13-20. (Map area F6)

Donalds E Jongelans - *Noorderkerkstraat 18, 624-6888*

You know when you walk into an old-style corner store and find a great pair of sunglasses in a dusty display case? That's what this store feels like, except it's not dusty. They have a fantastic selection of old (but not used) sunglasses and frames at reasonable prices. It's right behind the Noorderkerk, so you might want to stop in if you're at either of the markets held here (see Markets, above). Open: mon-sat 11-18. (Map area C3)

De Witte Tandenwinkel - *Runstraat 5, 623-3443*

I love the window of this store. They have the world's largest collection of toothbrushes! All shapes, all sizes and styles. They make unusual gifts, and they don't weigh much - which is a bonus when you're travelling. Take a look if you're in the neighbourhood, which has become known as the 9 streets. And if you want to splurge on something for someone special, check out the beautiful hand-made jewellery at Galerie Steimer, just two blocks away at Reestraat 25. I did. Open: mon 13-18; tues-fri 10-18; sat 10-17. (Map area C5)

Big Red Machine - *Waterlooplein 75*
http://www.hellsangelsamsterdam.nl

Here's a place where you can buy European biker mags, t-shirts, and this year's Hell's Angels calender. Upstairs is an Angels bar. Oh yeah, and I would heed the warning in the window - "This shop belongs to the Hells Angels Amsterdam. Fuck with it and find out." Open: tues-sat 12-17. (Map area E5)

Studio Spui - *Spui 4, 623-6926*

Check this shop for good specials on film close to its expiry date. Open: mon 10:30-18; tues-fri 09:30-18 (thurs 'til 21); sat 10-17:30. (Map area D5)

Photo Processing - *Kruidvat - Kalverstraat 187*

This is the cheapest place I know to get photos processed in Amsterdam. It takes two days and I had a roll of 24 colour prints done for ƒ12. Just a bit more expensive is the Dirk van den Broek supermarket at Heinekenplein. Photo booths, to have passport sized photos taken (ƒ7), can be found at the main post office (Singel 250), and at Central Station. (Map area D5)

Kinko's Copy Center - *Overtoom 62, 589-0910*

I'm not crazy about this joint because every time I've had some work done here they didn't do a good job. But they're open 24 hours a day, 7 days a week, so if you need to send a fax you can do it after 20:00, when phone rates are cheaper. (Map area A7)

Postcards

If you don't care whether Amsterdam is pictured on the ones you send home, look for the Boomerang *free* postcard racks. You'll find them in movie theatre lobbies, cafés and bars all around town.

HANGING OUT

This is the chapter for people who enjoy just wandering about the streets, seeing who's around, listening to music in the park, and for those of you who are really broke. During the warm months the streets and parks of Amsterdam come alive and you don't need a lot of money to find entertainment. I've also got a couple of suggestions for when it's rainy or cold.

PARKS

Amsterdam has many beautiful parks that are well used throughout the year, but particularly in the summer months when the sunset lingers for hours and the sky stays light 'til late. Picnics are very popular in Holland - you can invite all your friends at once, instead of just the small number that would otherwise fit in your apartment. After dark, however, it's best not to hang out in any of these parks alone.

Vondelpark

http://www.dds.nl/~park (a Dutch site, but with lots of nice photos)

When the weather is warm this is the most happening place in the city, especially on a Sunday. Crowds of people stroll through the park enjoying the sunshine and the circus-like atmosphere. Walk along the main pathways and notice the tarot and palm readers sitting peacefully in the shade of the trees. And all the jugglers practising with plates and balls and bowling pins, who look like jesters from a medieval court (especially if you've just had a smoke). Wander further into the park past old men fishing in quiet ponds and into the rose garden for an olfactory overload. Come out on the other side by a large field of cows and goats and even a couple of llamas! It's easy to forget you're in a city. About now you may want to look for one of the cafés in the park in order to buy an ice cream. Then listen to some music being performed in the band-shell, or to one of the dozens of musicians and bands jamming throughout the park. Look at the bright coloured parrots (I'm not kidding) in the trees. Play some footbag or frisbee. Watch the break-dancers. Or maybe you just want to join all the other people laying half-dressed on the grass, reading, smoking, playing chess, and sleeping. Trams: 1, 2, 5, 20. (Map area A8)

Amsterdamse Bos (Woods)

It's a bit of a trek to get out to this big patch of green, but what a gorgeous place. There are lots of winding bike and hiking paths, waterways, a gay cruising area, cafés, an open-air theatre, a Japanese garden complete with blooming cherry blossoms in the spring, and some wild parties when the weather is nice. In another part of the Bos is a big field where you can lie on your back and jets from nearby Schiphol fly really low right over you: not exactly peaceful, but I enjoy it! In the summer it's a great place to do mushrooms (see 'Shrooms, Shopping chapter). You can rent bikes here, and free maps and information are available from the Bosmuseum (on Koenenkade at the end of Bosbaan; 643-1414; open daily in the summer 10-17). Buses: 170, 171, 172.

Oosterpark (East Park)

Lots of ducks and lots of toddlers waddle around this park that's full of people strolling along the water and playing soccer in the big field. It also draws a lot of drummers (since that was banned in Vondelpark). The beautiful old band-shell is sometimes used for parties like the Oosterpark Festival in the first week of May, and the Roots Festival in June (*http://www.amsterdamroots.nl*). At the last couple of Holland Festivals (also in June; *http://www.hollandfestival.nl*) they set up huge screens in this park and broadcast live opera to crowds of picnickers. It's right by the Dappermarkt (see Shopping), and the Tropenmuseum. Tram 9. (Map G8)

Sarphatipark

This pretty little park is really close to the Albert Cuyp Market (see Markets, Shopping chapter), and Katsu and YoYo (see Coffeeshops, Cannabis chapter). If you get the fixings for a picnic you can go here to pig out and smoke. Trams 24, 25.

Wertheimpark

This small park is located on a canal just a couple of blocks away from the Waterlooplein flea market (see Markets, Shopping chapter) and it's an ideal place to cool your heels and catch your breath after battling the crowds. It's peaceful under the big trees by the water. It's just around the corner from Bakker Arend (see Bread, Food chapter). Tram 9. (Map area F6)

PUBLIC GARDENS & SQUARES

Gardens

The Begijnhof is a beautiful, old part of Amsterdam that should be seen. Look for an entrance behind the Amsterdam Historical Museum. There's also an entrance just off Spui Circle, through an arched doorway between Nieuwezijds Voorburgwal and the Esprit Café. Inside that entrance there's a plaque describing the interesting history of this pretty courtyard (Map area C6). In another part of town, the well-tended formal gardens behind the Rijksmuseum are pleasant, uncrowded places to sit and relax (they're accessible without a museum ticket). (Map area C8)

Leidseplein

I mention this square in the music chapter as a place to catch street musicians. If the weather is good there are also sure to be street performers who sometimes line up for their chance to entertain the throngs of tourists (and make some dough). A lot of these artists are very talented and you can see their professionalism as they work the crowds between each unicycling, fire-eating, juggling trick, and how they deal with the inevitable disruptive drunk. At the far end of the square, in front of the big movie theatre, are some cool, bronze lizard sculptures. And just across the street from there, carved high up on the marble pillars, is that age-old proverb "*Homo Sapiens Non Urinat In Ventum*", which is Latin for "don't piss in the wind". (Map area 7B)

Museumplein

Some of Holland's most famous museums are situated around this giant square, hence the name. They've had all kinds of problems with the recent renovations, but except for the underground parking garages and the crummy skate ramps, it looks pretty nice. The basketball courts are back if you want to shoot hoops. And there's an ice skating rink in the winter (*f*5 entry, *f*7 to rent skates). (Map area C8)

Dam Square

This huge, historic square in front of the palace has been completely renovated. It's quiet in the winter, but there's almost always something going on in the summer. Unfortunately, there are a lot of pickpockets and other sleazy creeps around here. Keep your eyes open and don't buy drugs from any of the scummy dealers: you'll definitely get ripped off. (Map area D4)

LIBRARIES

Public Library - *main branch Prinsengracht 587, 523-0900*
http://www.oba.nl

You have to be a member to borrow books, of course, but there's a lot to do here even if you're not. If you ask at the information desk inside they'll give you English newspapers and magazines like *Time* and *Newsweek* to read. They also have interesting photo exhibitions on the ground floor, and a row of computer terminals with free internet access. Computers can be reserved by phone or in person for a maximum of 30 minutes. In the small cafeteria, (where you can get a healthy sandwich and a fresh squeezed orange juice for just *f*5.25), you'll find more newspapers and magazines from around the world, many in English. On the first floor there's a good selection of English novels and any other section in the library will also have a lot of English books and magazines. Comics are also on the first floor. The travel section on the third floor has shelves of books about Holland and any other country you might be heading to. On the top floor is a music section with lots of magazines, and the CD collection with listening facilities. Finally, if you're looking for a flat or need to sell something, the bulletin board in the front entrance is well used. The collection at this library is still pretty good, but over the past few years the building has become increasingly crowded, dirty and under-staffed. And now you have to pay to use the toilets too! Open: mon-13-21; tues-thurs 10-21; fri/sat 10-17; sun (oct-mar only) 13-17. (Map area C6)

Pintohuis Library - *Sint Antoniesbreestraat 69, 624-3184*

In the early '70s, the city had plans to demolish this 17th century house in order to widen the street. Fortunately, it was saved by activists who squatted the building. After a complete restoration it was re-opened as a library. The little rooms, old wooden furniture and high ceilings covered with frescoes make it a wonderfully peaceful place to read or ponder for a while. Upstairs they have changing art exhibitions; the last one I saw was of erotic paintings. Open: mon, wed 14-20; fri 14-17; sat 11-14. (Map area E5)

INTERNET CAFÉS

ASCII (Amsterdam Subversive Code for Information Interchange)
Jodenbreestraat 24 (basement); http://www.squat.net/ascii

This is totally cool: a volunteer-run internet café in an old squat, set up by "an international bunch of iconoclasts, geeks, tech terrorists, squatters, eco-warriors, and anarchists". All the low-tech computers have been donated or picked from the garbage, and there's even a PC in the toilet so you can check your mail while you take a dump! Internet access is free, and the café serves very cheap drinks and snacks (like organic bananas). This friendly space is also used for workshops, experimental music performances (Sunday afternoons), political meetings, and pirate radio broadcasts. Open: daily 14-19. (Map area E6)

The Mad Processor - *Bloemgracht 82, 421-1482*

This is the place to visit if you feel like doing some gaming. Their 20 computers, which include some Macs, are set up in two rooms. There's a nice view of the canal from the front room and the back room, though larger, is cosy and sociable. Printers and scanners are also available. Gaming costs ƒ1.50 for 10 minutes, or ƒ7.50 an hour. Internet use costs ƒ1.50 for 10 minutes, or ƒ5 an hour. There's not so much available here in the way of food and beverages, but there's a candy machine to fuel your killing frenzies and they sell non-alcoholic drinks. Open: tues-sun 12-24. (Map area D4)

easyEverything - *Damrak 33, Reguliersbreestr. 22; http://www.easyeverything.com*

"The "world's largest internet cafés" are brought to you by the same super-rich guy who started easyJet and easyRentacar (see Getting Around). And for a corporate enterprise, the atmosphere at these places isn't too bad: it's bright and busy - even in the middle of the night - and you can always find a terminal. You buy a ticket with an ID number (good for 28 days or until you use up the time) to log on and off the computers. Prices start at ƒ5 which buys you a minimum of 40 minutes if the place is packed, and longer if less PCs are being used. You can scan, print, and download; use a web-cam to send a pic home to the family; or call long distance real cheap using PC to

5 AM in Amsterdam.

phone. They also sell drinks, brownies and other snacks (see All Night Eating, Food). The Damrak location is right by Central Station, and Reguliersbreestraat is by Rembrandtplein. Open: twenty-four seven.

SNOOKER & PING PONG

De Keizers Snooker Club - *Herengracht 256, 623-1586*

There's nowhere I know to play free snooker, but you can play here for ƒ10 an hour per table (no matter how many people are playing) and that's a pretty good deal. This price is valid daily 13 to 19:00. (Map area C5)

Tafeltennis Centrum Amsterdam - *Keizersgracht 209, 624-5780*

The free ping pong place in a squat that I wrote about in past editions is gone, so now it's pay to play again. This table tennis club charges ƒ14 an hour per table. They have a bar with food and drink, and the last time I was there they were playing old Rolling Stones. It's a neighbourhoody kind of place and there's often a table free, but to avoid disappointment you should probably call ahead to reserve. The entrance is a bit tricky to find. Walk down the hall, out the back door and across the courtyard. Open: mon-sat 16-1; sun 14-20. (Map area C5)

FREE CONCERTS

Het Concertgebouw - *Concertgebouwplein 2, 671-8345; www.concertgebouw.nl*

Every Wednesday at 12:30 this famous concert hall, world-renowned for it's acoustics, throws opens its doors to the proletariat for a free half-hour performance. These concerts are extremely popular so whether it's in the main hall (2000 seats) or the smaller one (500 seats), you should get there early.

Stopera Muziektheater - *Waterlooplein 22, 625-5455; http://www.stopera.nl*

Every Tuesday at 12:30 this modern concert hall, which is home to Amsterdam's ballet and opera, presents a free half-hour concert in its Boekman Zaal. It's also well-attended, so go early. Closed, however, in the summer months. (Map area E6)

Vondelpark Bandshell - *Vondelpark*

Free concerts are presented here in the summer (see Parks, this chapter). You'll find a schedule posted at the main entrance to the park. This is also where the Bike Wars demolition derby takes place (see Bikes, Getting Around chapter). (Map area A8)

SKATEBOARDING

Amsterdam's been without an indoor skatepark since the incredible 3rd Floor at the Vrieshuis Amerika was demolished. Hopefully, it won't be too long before they've re-established themselves as Skatepark Amsterdam at Kinetisch Noord (see Music chapter).

The two ramps at Museumplein are back, but they're not getting very good reviews. There's a giant half-pipe under the highway bridge by Flevopark. Take tram 14 to the end of the line, walk through the underpass and turn right. Along with the pipe, you'll also find some great graffiti. For more detailed info, stop in at Independent Outlet (see Shopping chapter), or Subliminal (Nieuwendijk 134, 428-2606) and they'll tell you what's up.

TOWER CLIMBING

Great views! Good exercise! Get off your ass!
Westerkerkstoren - *Westerkerk*. Open: apr-sept; mon-sat 10-16; ƒ3. The highest.
Zuiderkerkstoren - *Zuiderkerk*. Open: jun-sept; wed-sat 14-16; ƒ3.
Oudekerkstoren - *Oudekerk*. Open: jun-sept; wed-sat 14-16; ƒ3.
Beurs van Berlage - *Damrak 277*. Open: tues-sun 10-16; ƒ6.

NeMo - *Oosterdok 2*

I don't think this new science centre is worth the high admission price (see Museums), but if it's not too windy, the big public deck outside isn't a bad place to hang for a bit and look out over the city and the beautiful old boats in the surrounding docks. Just climb the big steps out front, and remember to take some munchies. Unfortunately, most of the year they're closed before sunset. Open: sun-thurs 10-18 ('til 21:00 in July and August); fri/sat 10-21. (Map area F3)

KITE FLYING & JUGGLING

Because it's flat and windy, Holland is a great country for kite flying, especially at the beach. They make some pretty cool, compact ones these days and a growing number of people are actually travelling with kites. Try Joe's Vliegerwinkel (Nieuwe Hoogstraat 19, 625-0139). They sell all kinds of kites, discs, and footbags, too! (Map area E5)

The Juggle Store (Kloveniersburgwal 54, 420-1980) is the place to find everything you need for juggling as well as info about juggling events around Holland and the rest of the world. They're open: tues-sat 12-17. (Map area E5)

SAUNAS

Sauna Fenomeen - *1e Schinkelstraat 14, 671-6780*

In spite of the fact that it's in a squat (now legalized), this health club is clean, modern, and well-equipped. People of all ages, shapes and sizes come here. When you enter, give your name and get a locker key from the reception booth on the right. On the left is a changing room with instructions and rules in both English and Dutch. You can bring your own towel or rent one there for ƒ1.50. Then get naked, have a shower, and try out the big sauna or the Turkish steam bath! There is also a café serving fresh fruit, sandwiches, juices and teas. It's a relaxing place to unwind and read the paper or just listen to music and veg. Also available at extra charges are massages, tranquillity tanks, and tanning beds. Monday is for women only, and the rest of the week is mixed. Thursday, Saturday and Sunday are smoke-free. The price, if you're finished before 18:00, is ƒ11. After that it's ƒ15. It's located just past the western end of Vondelpark. Open: daily 13-23. Closed for two months in the summer.

Marnixbad - *Marnixplein 9, 625-4843*

This place is a lot closer to the centre than Fenomeen. A sauna and shower costs ƒ12.75 or, if you want to swim too, ƒ15.50. Just a shower (without a sauna or swim) costs ƒ3. Bring your own towel. Thursday is for women only. Open: tues-sun 10-16 and 19-22:30. (Map area B3)

CEE-MENT PONDS

Zuiderbad - *Hobbemastraat 26, 678-1390*

90 years old. Beautifully restored. Naked swimming on Sundays. (Map area C8)

Mirandabad - *De Mirandalaan 9, 646-2522*

Indoor/outdoor. With whirlpool, wave machine, and tropical bath. South.

Flevoparkbad - Zeeburgerdijk 630, 692-5030

Heated outdoor pool. Open mid-may to early sept. East.

Bijlmerbad - *Bijlmerpark 76, 697-2501*

Disco swimming on Sunday afternoon. South-east.

Marnixbad - *Marnixplein 9, 625-4843*

See Saunas, above.

MUSEUMS

There are so many museums in this city that it could take you weeks to see them all. I'm only going to tell you about some of the more unusual and lesser-known collections. For basic information about the big ones - like the Rijksmuseum and the Van Gogh Museum - check the end of this chapter.

THE UNUSUAL ONES

The Sex Museum - *Damrak 18, 622-8376*

It's true that you could see almost everything that's on display here in the Red Light District for free, but admission is only ƒ4.50 and it's fun to tell your friends you went to the Sex Museum. I particularly like the pornography from the turn of the century. And the two 7-foot-high penis chairs where you can pose for photos. Don't forget your camera! Open: daily 10-23:30. (Map area E4)

The Erotic Museum - *Oudezijds Achterburgwal 54, 624-7303*

This collection is large (covers 5 floors) and varied, but unfortunately much of it is unlabelled. They have drawings by John Lennon, collages from Madonna's *Sex*, and a very ugly, very funny, pornotoon from Germany. You can also push a button that sets a dozen or so vibrators into action! There is a floor of hard-core videos and phone sex, and above that a rather tame S/M room. There's only one reference to gay male sex in the entire museum, however, a surprising omission considering Amsterdam's status as the gay capital of Europe. Admission: ƒ5. Open: daily 11-1. (Map area E4)

The Hash Marihuana Hemp Museum - *Oudezijds Achterburgwal 130, 623-5961*

While this museum used to be simply a required stop on every smoker's list of places to visit, it's matured into an informative collection for anyone who's interested in alternative forms of energy, medicine or agriculture. The exhibit, which is now located in the building that used to house the Tattoo Museum, consists of photos, documents, videos and artifacts dealing with all aspects of the amazing hemp plant: history, medicinal uses and cannabis culture. There's even a grow room. And if you're hungry for more info you can peruse their small reference library or pick up one of the free pamphlets on hemp and its uses that you'll find by the entrance. They also sell books, magazines, and hemp products (including seeds). Visitors who do smoke will be interested in meeting Eagle Bill, the guy who really popularized the Vaporizer. He's often there, demonstrating how it works. The vaporizer is a glass waterpipe that uses a powerful heat source to "vaporize" the THC-bearing resin without actually burning the weed in the bowl. It's a healthy alternative to filling your lungs with smoke, *and* it gets you wasted! He'll give you a free taste, but you should definitely make a small donation. Located in the Red Light District. Admission: ƒ12. Open: daily 11-22. (Map area E5)

The Torture Museum - *Singel 449, 320-6642*

Don't leave Amsterdam without visiting this unique collection of torture instruments. It's very educational. You'll learn where expressions like "putting the pressure on" originated. The museum is nicely laid out in an old house and lit with dingy, dungeon lighting. Each object has a small plaque explaining its function, and by and on whom it was inflicted. Detailed drawings illustrate their use. If you aren't already aware of Christianity's bloody history this is the place to see, quite graphically, just what has been done to people in the name of "god". (And speaking of god, what do you get when you cross an agnostic, an insomniac, and a dyslexic? Someone who stays up all night wondering if there's a dog.) Admission: adults ƒ7.50; students ƒ5.50. Open: daily 10-23. (Map area E4)

Tropenmuseum - *Linnaeusstraat 2, 568-8215; http://www.kit.nl/tropenmuseum*

This is one of the big ones that's in every guidebook. I'm including it here because it's such an amazing place, yet many visitors choose to skip it. This beautiful old building in eastern Amsterdam houses a fantastic collection of artifacts and exhibits from and about the developing world. The permanent exhibition uses model villages, music, slide shows, and lots of push-button, hands-on displays to give you a feel for everyday life in these countries. There are also changing exhibitions in the central hall and in the photo gallery. At the entrance you'll find listings for films and music in the adjoining Souterijn theatre (see Film chapter), but they're not included in the admission price. Admission: adults ƒ10 to ƒ12.50; students ƒ5 to ƒ7.50. Open: mon-fri 10-17; sat/sun 12-17. (Map area H7)

De Poezeboot (Cat Boat) - *a houseboat on the Singel opposite #20, 625-8794*

Attention cat lovers! This isn't really a museum, but what the fuck? Spend some time on this boat playing with dozens of love-hungry stray cats who now have a home thanks to donations from the public and volunteers who help out here. The boat is free to visit, but you're expected to make a contribution on your way out. Grab a postcard for your cat back home. Open: daily 13-16. (Map area D3)

Electric Ladyland - The First Museum of Florescent Art
2e Leliedwarsstraat 5, 420 3776; http://www.electric-lady-land.com

It took 7 years to complete this very tiny, very trippy museum in the basement of this small shop, and when you see it you'll know why. It includes an intricate cave-like environment where you can push buttons that light up different areas of the space and play Jimi Hendrix. There are also display cases where minerals and fluorescent artifacts from all over the world are displayed under lights of different wavelengths, revealing startling, hidden colours. A ƒ5 donation gets you an informative booklet and access to the collection. Open Tuesday through Saturday in the afternoon, or by appointment. (Map area B4)

Woonboot Museum (Houseboat Museum) - *across from Prinsengr. 296, 427-0750*
http://www.houseboatmuseum.nl

The 84-year-old ship housing this museum will show you what it's like to live on one of Amsterdam's approximately 2500 houseboats. There are also scale models of other boats, photos, a slide show, and displays intended to answer all those questions you have about life on the canals. Admission: ƒ4.75. Open: wed-sun 11-17 (mar-oct); fri-sun 11-17 (nov-feb). (Map area C5)

Heineken Brewery Museum - *Stadhouderskade 78, 523-9436*

I used to recommend this place, but the price has gone up to ƒ11, it's no longer a working brewery, nor do they offer all-you-can-drink; so I'm not sure why you'd want to go there now. Open: tues-sat 10-17. Trams: 16, 24, 25. (Map area D8)

Condom Museum - *Warmoesstraat 141, 627-4174*
http://www.condomerie.com

This tiny museum is made up of a colourful assortment of condom packages from around the world. The display is housed in a small glass case in the Condomerie (see Sex Chapter). It doesn't take long to view the collection, but checking out the names and logos on the boxes (like the camouflage condom - "don't let them see you coming") is good for a laugh. Open: mon-sat 11-17. (Map area D4)

The Smallest House In Amsterdam - *Singel 7*

The front of this house is only 1.01 metres wide! Property taxes were based on the width of the front of the house when this one was built, so they were pretty clever. You can't go inside, but it's still cool to take a look if you're walking by. It's not a museum. People live there. I used to know somebody who lived in the third smallest house in Amsterdam. She hated it when tourists would knock on her door to ask if they could look around the third littlest house in Amsterdam, so don't do it. There are other tiny houses around, including: Haarlemmerstraat 43 (1.28 metres wide); Oude Hoogstraat 22 (2.02 metres wide); and Singel 166 (1.84 metres wide). (Map area D3)

Botanical Gardens (Hortus Botanicus) - *Plantage Middenlaan 2A, 625-8411*
www.hortus-botanicus.nl

Established in 1638, this is one of the oldest Botanical Gardens in the world. The collection includes thousands of species of plants and they're displayed in a wonderful variety of greenhouses and landscaped gardens. The largest building has both desert and rainforest environments, but my favourite is still the palm house - a beautiful old building. You'll find peyote in the cactus greenhouse and the butterfly room is also quite exciting. The café, the Orangerie, is very pleasant - full of plants and little birds hunting for crumbs lodged in the wicker chairs. Occasionally, classical music is performed live. Open: mon-fri 9-17; sat/sun 11-17 (oct-apr 'til 16). ƒ10. Trams: 7, 9, 14. (Map area F6)

National Trade Union Museum (Vakbonds Museum) - *Henri Polaklaan 9,*
624-1166; http://www.fnv.nl/~Vakbondsmuseum

In the late 1800's, the famous architect Hendrik Berlage was commissioned to design the head office for the General Dutch Diamond Cutters Union. That union was the first in The Netherlands to win its workers the right to a vacation, and the first in the world to attain an eight-hour working day! The building is beautiful and it's fitting that it now houses this museum of the Dutch trade union movement. Most of the exhibits, which include displays about union activities of the past and present, are in Dutch, but a free English guide is available at the front desk. It kind of makes you want to get out your old, scratchy Woody Guthrie albums. Admission is ƒ3 for card-carrying union members and ƒ5 for the unorganized. Take tram 9 to Plantage Kerklaan. Open: tues-fri 11-17; sun 13-17. (Map area F6)

Open Monument Day - *early September (8 & 9 in 2001), throughout Holland*
http://www.openmonumentendag.nl

On Open Monument Day over 3000 historical monuments in Holland - homes, windmills, courtyards, churches - that usually aren't accessible to the public, open their doors. On this day you can pop into any building that flies a flag with a key on it. For more info call 627-7706 or visit their site.

Eyeglass Museum (Brilmuseum) - *Gasthuismolensteeg 7, 421-2414*
http://www.brilmuseumamsterdam.nl

I thought this museum sounded kind of interesting - a history of eyeglasses on display in an early 17th century house. But my curiosity wasn't strong enough to warrant the ƒ10 admission. Some of you 4-eyes might want to take a peek, though. Open: wed-sat 12-18. (Map area C5)

Vrolijk Museum - *Meibergdreef 15, 566-9111 (beeper 841)*

I haven't been here either, but listen to this: an 18th and 19th century collection of some professor and his son's embryological and anatomical specimens! Weird. It's out of the way in south-east Amsterdam and visits are by appointment only. Have a good time; I'm off to watch *Frankenhooker* again.

THE BIG ONES

Here is some basic information on Amsterdam's biggest and most famous museums. They all have impressive collections and can get quite crowded during peak season. Once a year there's a **Museum Weekend** - when all the big ones are free. In 2002 it's on April 13 & 14; in 2003 it's on April 12 & 13.

A **Museum Card** - good for one year - costs ƒ70 (ƒ30 if you're under 25!) and is available at most of these museums. It gets you in free or at a substantial discount to almost all the big ones in Holland. If you're planning to go to more than a few of these, are visiting other cities in

Under the Rijksmuseum.

The Netherlands, or are returning within a year, then it's a good deal. The size of the discount that the card entitles you to varies considerably from museum to museum and show to show, but the visit at which you purchase the card is always free; so if you're smart you'll check the current discount rates and buy your card at the museum where you'd otherwise have to pay the highest surcharge.

The **Museum Nacht** (*http://www.de-n8.nl*) is a very cool happening that was so successful last year that it'll probably become a regular event. Thirty-three museums in Amsterdam opened up after-hours and provided visitors with unconventional atmospheres in which to view the collections. The Stedelijk Museum was transformed into a club lounge, there was line dancing in the Rijksmuseum, and the Botanical Gardens offered a tour of the hallucinogenic plants in their collection. The ƒ25 Museum Night pass included entrance to the museums as well as transport by tram, bus and boat - a great deal. When the next one is announced, I'll post it on the Get Lost! Website: *http://www.xs4all.nl/~getlost.*

Rijksmuseum - *Stadhouderskade 42, 674-7000 ; http://www.rijksmuseum.nl*
Home to 20 Rembrandts. Open: daily 10-17. ƒ17.50; 18 and under, free.
Trams: 2, 5, 6, 7, 10, 20. (Map area C8)

Vincent van Gogh Museum - *Paulus Potterstr. 7,570-5200; www.vangoghmuseum.nl*
Open: daily 10-18. ƒ15.50; 17 and under, ƒ5. Trams: 2, 3, 5, 12, 20. (Map area B8)

Anne Frank House - *Prinsengracht 263, 556-7100; http://www.annefrank.nl*
Open: daily 9-19 (apr-aug 31 'til 21). ƒ12.50; 17 and under, ƒ5. Trams: 13, 14, 17, 20.
(Map area C4)

Stedelijk Museum - *Paulus Potterstraat 13, 573-2737; http://www.stedelijk.nl* .
Modern art. Open: daily 11-17. ƒ12.50; 16 and under, ƒ7.50. Trams: 2, 3, 5, 12, 16. (Map
area B8)

Rembrandt House - *Jodenbreestraat 4-6, 520-0400; http://www.rembrandthuis.nl*
Open: mon-sat 10-17; sun 13-17. ƒ15; 16 and under, ƒ2.50. Trams: 9, 14. (Map area E6)

Amsterdam Historical Museum - *Kalverstraat 92, 523-1822; http://www.ahm.nl*
Open: mon-fri 10-17; sat/sun 11-17. ƒ13.50; 16 and under, ƒ6.75. Trams: 1, 2, 5, 11.
(Map area D5)

Jewish Historical Museum - *J. Daniël Meyerplein 2-4, 626-9945; http://www.jhm.nl*
Open: daily 11-17. ƒ10; students, ƒ6.50. 17 and under, ƒ4.50. Trams: 9, 14, 20. (Map
area E6)

Portuguese Synagogue - *Mr. Visserplein 3, 624-5351*
Open: sun-fri 10-16. ƒ7.50. Trams: 9, 14, 20. (Map area E6)

WW2 Resistance Museum (Verzetsmuseum) - *Plantage Kerklaan 61, 620-2535*
http://www.verzetsmuseum.org
Open: mon 12-17; tues-fri 10-17; sat/sun 12-17. ƒ9. Trams: 4, 12, 25. (Map area F6)

Hidden Church (Amstelkring) - *Oudezijds Voorburgwal 40, 624-6604*
http://www.museumamstelkring.nl
Open: mon-sat 10-17; sun 13-17. ƒ7.50; students, ƒ6. (Map area E4)

Maritime Museum (Scheepvaartmuseum) - *Kattenburgerplein 1, 523-2222*
http://www.scheepvaartmuseum.nl
Open: tues-sun 10-17; (in summer, mon 10-17). ƒ14.50; 17 and under, ƒ8. Buses: 22,
32. (Map area F5)

NeMo (Science Centre) - *Oosterdok 2, 531-3233; http://www.newmet.nl*
Open: tues-sun 10-17. ƒ18.75. Bus 22. (Map area F5)

Kröller-Müller Museum - *Hoge Veluwe National Park, 031-859-1041 / 031-859-1241*
www.kmm.nl
This museum is located in the middle of a huge park in the middle of Holland. It
has a big, incredibly trippy sculpture garden and a fantastic collection of Van Gogh's.
Free use of bikes on site. Should be experienced. The park is open during daylight
hours; the museum: tues-sun 10-17. Admission to the park and the museum is ƒ20 (to
the park alone - ƒ10); and parking costs ƒ8.50.

MUSIC

Many guidebooks say that Amsterdam doesn't have a "world class" music scene, unlike some of its neighbouring capital cities. What a load of shit, but that shouldn't come as a surprise with a yuppie phrase like "world class". In fact, even if you're only here for a couple of days you should be able to find all kinds of music. From community-run squats and old churches to dance halls and large clubs, this city is full of great venues and great musicians.

Note: The government here just unleashed a fucked-up new tax law that makes it very difficult for small bars and clubs to hire bands. One great venue for new acts, the Winston Kingdom (see below), has already had to stop presenting live music. There is opposition to the law, and hopefully changes will be made.

HOW TO FIND OUT WHO'S PLAYING

A.U.B. - *Leidseplein 26, 0900-0191 (f.75/min); http://www.uitlijn.nl*
The Amsterdams Uitburo (AUB) is the place to start a search into who's playing in town. You'll find listings of all the music happening in and around the city on display here as well as the schedules for the Paradiso, the Melkweg (see below), and the other bars and clubs that feature live music. There are also racks full of flyers and info about theatre and film. It's convenient to buy advance tickets here, in person or by phone, but there's an expensive service charge (about f4 per ticket). Buying them directly from the venues, or from record stores, will usually save you a couple of guilders. Open: daily 10-18 (thurs 'til 21). (Map area C7)

Shark - *http://www.underwateramsterdam.com*
This popular English-language fanzine is a great source of info on what's happening at music spots around the city - alternative venues as well as mainstream. It appears every two weeks and can be picked up for free at cool shops, bars, and the AUB. It also features short articles, reviews, horoscopes, and queer info. Check out their web site for a searchable database of current events.

Way-Out: Alternative Lijst
I don't know who publishes this one-page flyer, but I'm glad they do. It includes music listings for squat clubs and alternative movie theatres. Look for it in bars and in restaurants like Zaal 100 (see Restaurants, Food chapter).

Irie Reggae Web Site - *http://www.irielion.com/irie*
If you're into reggae, look up this comprehensive listing of reggae bands and sound systems playing around Holland.

LIVE MUSIC / PARTY VENUES

Paradiso - *Weteringschans 6-8, 626-4521*
http://www.paradiso.nl
I wanted to go to this concert hall since I was 14 and bought the album *Link Wray Live at the Paradiso*. Now I go all the time! Located in a beautiful old church, this is

an awesome place to see live music. There's a big dance floor with a balcony around it. Upstairs and in the basement, are smaller halls where different bands sometimes jam after the main event. This is also a great venue for parties and performance art. I've seen everything from balloons filled with joints dropping from the ceiling to a live sex performance piece. Musicians seem to love this place, and big name bands will often do gigs here if they're touring Europe. Tickets here and at the Melkweg (see below) almost always go on sale 3 weeks before the show, and range in price from about ƒ10 to ƒ30. In addition, they charge a membership fee of ƒ5, which buys you a card that's valid for one month. If you're going to a sold out show it's a good idea to buy your membership in advance to avoid a long line-up at the door. Located just a stone's throw from Leidseplein. (Map area C7)

Melkweg (Milky Way) - *Lijnbaansgracht 234, 624-1777*
http://www.melkweg.nl

The Melkweg is located in a big warehouse (which used to be a dairy), on a canal just off Leidseplein. Although it's not the cheapest venue in town, there's so much to do inside that you get your money's worth. Prices are about the same as the Paradiso and they also charge a membership fee of ƒ5. Most nights you'll find bands playing in the old hall, or in the new, bigger, "Max" (revoltingly named after its corporate sponsor, some crappy soft-drink). Also on the ground floor is a photo gallery, and a bar/restaurant. (Entry to the gallery is free via the restaurant entrance on Marnixstraat from Wednesday to Sunday, 14 to 20:00.) Unfortunately, the rest of the building is often closed now, but if it isn't, explore the upstairs and you'll find a video room that shows all different kinds of stuff from Annie Sprinkle and Sonic Youth to underground footage that you'd never find anywhere else. There is also a playhouse for live theatre (which is often in English), and a cinema (see Film chapter). Flyers listing Melkweg events are available by the front door of the club (even when it's closed). The box office is open from 19:30 on every night that there's a show and: mon-fri 13-17; sat/sun 16-18. (Map area C7)

OCCII (Onafhankelijk Cultureel Centrum In It) - *Amstelveenseweg 134, 671-7778*
http://www.occii.org

This cool squat club has been open for more than 15 years. There's always something going on here: live music of all types, cabarets, readings, and other happenings. Their small hall has a bar, a nice-sized stage, and a dance floor. It has a divey, comfortable atmosphere. Back by the entrance, an old stairway leads to the Kasbah café on the second floor. The music and crowds are diverse and fun. Admission is usually ƒ5 to ƒ10. Look for posters advertising their events or wander by. The complex also houses a sauna (see Saunas, Hanging Out chapter). It's located at the far side of Vondelpark, across the street and to the left. They usually close for a while in the summer. Tram 2.

Academie (O.T. 3:01) - *Overtoom 301, 779-4913*
http://squat.net/overtoom301

Despite pressure to have the resident squatters evicted by those who would rather see this building rot than be used for non-profit purposes, volunteers have managed to create one of the most important cultural centres in the city on this site. The Academie (so named because it formerly housed a film academy) was sitting empty until a bunch of squatters moved in, fixed it up, and made it available to the public. Now new projects are being launched here all the time. There's a restaurant/bar (see De Peper, Food chapter), a movie theatre (see Film), a darkroom, and studios which are used for dance, performance and workshops. There are also some great parties happening in both the restaurant and the big studios. DJs play regular gigs, like the Dub Club 100, and musicians perform all styles of music. It's underground Amsterdam at its accessible best. Look for a copy of *Shark* or the *Way Out List* (see above) for their schedule. Tram 1. (Map area A7)

A NOTE ABOUT SQUATTING IN AMSTERDAM

If a building in Amsterdam remains empty for more than a year without the owner putting it to some use, it can be squatted. This law is meant to protect the city from speculators who sit on their property while prices rise due to the severe housing shortage.

That doesn't mean that squatters have an easy time taking over a building. The legal definition of occupancy is a slippery one, and it's difficult to have a building defined as vacant. In addition, a great deal of work is usually needed to make a squat habitable and often legal battles ensue.

I have a lot of respect for those who have chosen to live as squatters as an expression of their political beliefs. They are simultaneously working to preserve and create housing in this overcrowded city. Several of these organised squats have opened restaurants and clubs that are among the best in Amsterdam. Many of them live under imminent threat of being forced out by banks and developers. Going to these squats is a way of showing your support for a creative, co-operative way of living as well as your opposition to conservative pigs who care more about money than people. For more information about squatting look online at http://squat.net. And for up-to-date info about events in squats, check out the excellent and easy-to-use database at http://radar.squat.net

H******n Music Hall - *Arena Boulevard 590, 409-7900, or 0900-300-1250 (f.99/min)*
Since we have no real say in where our tax guilders go, it was left to a corporation to fund the building of this new music hall. Enter Heineken. The idea is to bring bands to Amsterdam that draw more people than the clubs in the city can handle. Anyway, it's brand new, holds 5500 people, and the acoustics are supposed to be out of this world. It'll be worth looking into who's playing here while you're in town. It's located way out by the Amsterdam Arena stadium - from Central Station take the Metro to Amsterdam Bijlmer and it's just a few minutes walk.

Maloe Melo - *Lijnbaansgracht 163, 420-4592*
http://www.maloemelo.nl
They call this place the "home of the blues", but you're just as likely to catch a band playing punk, country, or rock. There's live music here every night and no cover charge. Walk to the back of the bar and you'll find the entrance to another room where the stage is. Don't be shy to push your way up to the front where there's a bit more space. This is a good spot to check out local talent. And if the band is bad, you can wander next door and see what's happening at the Korsakoff (see Bars). The bar is open from 21:00 (music room from 22:30) until 3 on weeknights, and 4 on the weekends. Trams: 7, 10, 13, 14, 17. (Map area B5)

Winston Kingdom - *Warmoesstraat 123-129, 623-1380*
http://www.winston.nl

There's all sorts of great stuff happening here at this old hotel and club: parties, poetry, art exhibitions. Unfortunately, the new tax law (see above) has forced them to stop booking live bands, but it's still a lively, fun spot. As well as regular long-running events like the popular trash-glam Club Vegas, there are lounge nights, rap and hip-hop, disco parties, and they've got a lot of plans for the future. Cover is usually *f*5 to *f*10. Located in the Red Light District. The entrance is just to the right of the hotel. Open: sun-thurs 20-3; fri/sat 20-4. (Map area D4)

Bimhuis - *Oude Schans 73-77, 623-1361*
http://www.bimhuis.nl

For more than 25 years this is where jazz lovers have been gathering. I find the actual hall a bit uncomfortable, though it's intimate, and the sound is excellent. Ticket prices average *f*15 to *f*30 and some hot musicians have played here. On Tuesdays they host jam sessions, and admission is free. Other spots around town with *free* live jazz include Bourbon Street (Leidsekruisstraat 6, 623-3440), Alto Jazz (Korte Leidsedwarsstraat 115, 626-3249) and Casablanca (see below). Concerts at the Bimhuis start at 21:00 on Thursday through Saturday nights. (Map area E5)

Casablanca - Zeedijk 26, 625-5685

It's well past it's heyday as a famous jazz club, and a small beer will set you back *f*4, but there's no cover charge to hear live jazz here on Sunday through Wednesday nights. On the weekends there's karaoke. And every first Sunday of the month it's Finger-poppin' Soul - a nine-hour marathon of soul music! The DJ's start at about 16:00 and by evening the little dance floor is packed with a slightly older crowd who know how rare it is to hear these tunes in Amsterdam clubs. Open: sun-wed 20-3; thurs-sat 20-4. (Map area E4)

The Last Waterhole - *Oudezijds Armsteeg 12, 624-4814*
http://www.lastwaterhole.nl

Tucked away in a little alley in the Red Light District, this old bar has seen more than its share of live music over the years. It's a rock-and-blues-jam-session, Grateful-Dead-cover-band kind of place. Somewhere to catch local groups, like soul/funksters Jerome Lee City. Bands play every night (except Monday) at 22:00, and there's no cover charge. They have a very good sound system, but for some reason they recently took out the couches and chairs and replaced them with really uncomfortable benches. And just in case you were wondering, the electric fans whirling away in the washrooms are to stop people from doing coke. Open: sun-thurs 11-2; fri/sat 11-4. (Map area B4)

AMP - *KNSM Laan 13, 418-1111*
http://www.ampstudios.nl

A lot of musicians hang out at the bar in this rehearsal space. There's often live music on the weekends, especially Sundays when it's usually jazz. During their "battle of the bands", it's a good place to check out local talent. They also host parties - Goa trance, salsa, African. The rest of the week it's super mellow, and if you find yourself way the fuck out here amidst all the condo developments on KNSM island, it's the coolest place to stop in and get a cup of tea or a beer, and maybe shoot a game of pool. Also in the area are: End of the World (see Restaurants, Food chapter) and the Azart Ship (see Bars). Admission to AMP, when there's a band, is around ƒ5 to ƒ15. Open: sun-thurs 12-1; fri/sat 12-3. From Central Station take bus 32 or 59.(direction KNSM Eiland), or night bus 79 (ask the driver to let you off at Azartplein). (Map area I3)

Inrichting Alternative Dance Night - *Overtoom 301*
http://come.to/deinrichting

Two studios at the squatted film academie (O.T.3:01, see above) provide the latest home for this bi-monthly gathering of goths, vampires and everyone else who likes to dress all in black when they go out dancing. The music ranges from industrial to neofolk to noise, and the organizers go out of their way to create a genuinely gothic environment. Often there are live performances. In the past it's been held every second Saturday of the month. Admission is ƒ8.50. Open: 22-4. (Map area A7)

Cave of Satyr - *Haarlemmerstraat 118*
http://www.geocities.com/thecaveofsatyr

Here's another one for the vampire set. This one is located in the basement of Du Lac (see Bars), but it has it's own entrance. It's been described as "a chill space for Goths", with a couple of little rooms away from the dancing where you can relax and have a conversation without screaming over the music. It happens once a month, on the first Friday, and admission is ƒ7.50. To find out about other parties around town, stop by the goth café Legendz (Kinkerstraat 45, 683-8513; *www.legendz.nl*). Cave of Satyr open: 22-5. (Map area D3)

King Shiloh Sound System - *Various Locations*
http://www.shashamani.co.uk/shiloh/introshiloh.htm

The organizers of this reggae sound system have been around for years and along with presenting dances on a regular basis, they also have a record label and a show on pirate Radio 100 (see Pirate Radio, below). They do regular gigs at OCCII (see above) and after most big reggae shows. Admission is usually about ƒ7.50. Check the Irie Web Site (see above) for more info. Stay Positive.

Volta - *Houtmankade 336, 682-6429*

Lately, parties have been occurring every Friday night at this west-side cultural centre. The building's not too big, which makes for a nice, intimate atmosphere, while the high ceilings give some breathing space on a crowded night. Recently there've been DJs spinning hip-hop, ragga, jungle, and raï to a pretty young crowd. There's often live music of some sort on Thursday nights, and if you're travelling with an instrument, swing by for their Wednesday night jam sessions. Admission to Volta is usually a very reasonable ƒ5. (Map area B1)

Westergasfabriek - *Haarlemmerweg 8-10, 581-0425*
http://www.westergasfabriek.nl

This old factory complex consists of 15 industrial monuments and their surrounding grounds. The site hosts music and film festivals, parties, and performances. When its current renovations are completed it will continue to host all sorts of cultural events, as well as providing additional parkland for Amsterdam's west side. This is also the home of West Pacific (488-7778; *http://www.westpacific.nl*), a restaurant that hosts popular dance nights every weekend. (Map area A1)

Akhnaton - *Nieuwezijds Kolk 25, 624-3396*
http://www.akhnaton.nl

Well-known for their African and Latin American music nights, Akhnaton also features hip-hop parties, roots ragga nights and the occasional jazz/funk jam. African and salsa nights tend to draw a more smartly-dressed crowd than I'm used to, and it's a bit of a pick-up scene, but the music is really good. It's only a five minute walk from Central Station. Open most Friday and Saturday nights. Admission is usually about ƒ10 to ƒ15. (Map area D4)

Club Arena - *'s-Gravesandestraat 51, 694-7444*
http://www.hotelarena.nl

They stopped booking bands here a few years ago which was a real shame - the 400 capacity hall is roomy and comfortable with space to dance and space to watch. But they still have regular dance nights, with DJs spinning trip-hop on one night and music from the '70s or '80s on another. Guests staying here (see Hotels, Places to Sleep) get a discount. Personally, I'm hoping they'll bring back the bands. Trams: 3, 6, 14. (Map area G8)

Panama - *Oostelijke Handelskade 4, 311-8686*
http://www.panama.nl

The little organic fruit and vegetable market that used to be here got the boot so this new club, theatre and restaurant could open. The beautiful old building it's in has been completely renovated and it looks great. There's dancing here 5 nights a week (latin, jazz, disco) with a steep entry of ƒ20. Maybe this will turn into a hip place, but it's more likely to be a hangout for all the yuppies moving into this old harbour district. (Map area I4).

Theater de Cameleon - *3e Kostverlorenkade 35, 489-4656*

Located at the far end of Vondelpark, Theater de Cameleon hosts non-commercial, alternative performances. They present plays, occasionally a stand-up comic, and regular open mike nights for music. At their monthly Club Cameleon evening, there's an open stage with comedy, street theatre, performance art, and anything else anyone wants to do. It's more of a Dutch scene, but there's still usually some English spoken, and it's always a laugh. Call ahead if you'd like to perform. Admission is free for the open music stage, and ƒ5 to ƒ15 for other events.

ADM - *Hornweg 6-8, 411-0081*
http://www.contrast.org/adm

This huge building along the harbour west of Amsterdam was squatted a few years ago after sitting empty for 5 years. Their opening party featured performances by Bettie Serveert (who played a fantastic set of Velvet Underground covers), and The Ex. Every party I've been to here has been great. And because the owner of the building is an evil little fucker, the effort you make to get out here will be especially appreciated. If you're not up to the long bike ride, there's usually a shuttle bus that leaves from behind Central Station when they have a party. They also serve a vegetarian meal in their café every Friday and Sunday from 18:00. The cost is ƒ10. Call to reserve and for directions.

Kinetisch Noord - *NDSM-terrein, T.T. Neveritaweg, Amsterdam North, 330-5480
http://www.ndsm.nl*

After forcibly closing most of the affordable spaces for artists (and their audiences) in the centre, the city council may fund a complex on the site of an old wharf that's been squatted in North Amsterdam - far from any real estate that's currently of interest to their developer friends. Cynicism aside, it sounds pretty cool. There are plans for cheap studios, performance spaces, a cinema, galleries, a skatepark and a café and restaurant. Although it's quite a trek to get out to this industrial area, the view over the water is gorgeous. I'll post more info on the Get Lost! website.

DANCE CLUBS

If you're into dance clubs, raves and parties, refer back to Club Fashions in the Shopping chapter: those stores all have party information. Clubs usually open at about 23:00 and close around 4 or 5:00. Most have a dress code.

Mazzo - *Rozengracht 114, 626-7500; http://www.mazzo.nl*
Relaxed and friendly. Open: wed-sun. (Map area B4)

Club More - *Rozengracht 133, 528-7459; http://www.expectmore.nl*
Trendy and cool. Some women-only nights. Open: wed-sun. (Map area B4)

iT - *Amstelstraat 24, 625-0111; http://www.it.nl*
Gay disco. (Map area E6)

De Trut - *Bilderdijkstraat 156*
Gay (mixed). In a legalized squat. Admission is only f2.50. Sunday nights only. Doors open at 23:00 and close at 23:30. (Map area A6)

Time - *Nieuwezijds Voorburgwal 163, 423-3792*
Near Dam Square. (Map area D5)

Escape - *Rembrandtplein 11, 622-1111; http://www.escape.nl*
Popular, especially on Saturday. Open: thurs-sun. (Map area E6)

Sinners in Heaven - *Wagenstraat 3-7, 620-1375; http://www.sinners.nl*
Trendy. (Map area E6)

Soul Kitchen - *Amstelstraat 32, 620-2333*
Disco, r&b, maybe some soul. (Map area E6)

Marcanti Plaza - *Jan van Galenstraat 6-10, 682-3456*
Big place with dancing on Friday and Saturday nights.

Dansen bij Jansen - *Handboogstraat 11, 620-1779 ; http://www.dansenbijjansen.nl*
Students. (Map area D6)

Odeon - *Singel 460, 624-9711; http://www.odeontheater.nl*
More students. 3 floors. (Map area C6)

STREET MUSIC

Take a walk around Amsterdam on any warm day (and some cold ones!) and you'll find street musicians everywhere. Popular areas for people to play include Dam Square, Leidseplein, Max Euweplein, Central Station and Vondelpark (which also has a big free stage in the summer). If I stop and listen for awhile I always give a guilder or two, which I think is a pretty good deal for having someone liven up the streets and people of a city.

Robin Nolan Trio jamming in Leidseplein.

RADIO

Radio 100 - *98.3FM*
http://www.radio100.nl

This pirate radio station has been around since 1986, and it's the biggest independent radio station in Amsterdam. They broadcast a wide range of shows covering many subjects and all types of sounds. They play an outstanding selection of music from around the world. Their schedule is listed in *Shark* (see above) and they also broadcast online.

Radio de Vrije Keyser - *96.3FM*
http://www.xs4all.nl/~keyser

Born out of the radical squat movement of the late-seventies, these old-timers on the pirate scene became famous for their diverse, sometimes crazy programming. They broadcast a mix of politics, squat news, and punk music every Tuesday from 14 to 20:00, and they're often on the scene, broadcasting live, from demonstrations and squat evictions around town. They also have a great TV show on Amsterdam 1 on Saturday nights.

Radio Patapoe - *97.3FM*
http://www.desk.nl/~ptp

Power to the pirates. Diverse programming (when they're on the air), since 1989, featuring all kinds of cool music. All with no commercials. Yes!

BBC World Service - *648AM*
http://www.BBC.co.uk/worldservice

Various shows, but best of all, news in English every hour on the hour.

FESTIVALS

All year long there are festivals going on in and around Amsterdam. Most of the ones I've listed are free. For any without precise dates, check with the tourist office.

Queen's Day - *April 30, everywhere in Holland*

The biggest and best party of the year happens on this day in celebration of the Queen's birthday (though it's actually her mother's birthday, because Beatrix's birthday is in January - a bad time for an outdoor party). Amsterdam becomes one big, orange-coloured carnival, with music and dancing and gallivanting and carousing. The world's biggest flea market opens for business: almost anything can be bought or sold. And despite the ridiculous new rules and regulations imposed by the city council over the last couple of years, it's still unbelievably fun. Type "Queen's Day Amsterdam" into any search engine and you'll find hundreds of photos.

Bevrijdingsdag - *May 5, Dam Square, Amsterdam*

This one celebrates Holland's liberation from the Nazis at the end of WW2: something worth celebrating. If you're interested in seeing some of the country's bigger bands, check this out. It's always a fun party. Fuck Nazis!

Legalize Street Party - *late May / early June (June 2nd in 2001), Amsterdam*
http://www.legalize.org

I never miss this annual street rave protesting the global war on drugs. The meeting place is usually at Dam Square. Then there's a lively dance through the town and out of the city centre (because the cops get nervous when the streets are liberated) to a place where all the sound-systems and their DJs can set up for the party. On the same day street raves take place in cities all over the world.

Ruigoord Festival - *June 21, Ruigoord*
http://www.ruigoord.nl

Over twenty-five years ago this town just west of Amsterdam was squatted and turned into a very cool community of artists and free-thinkers. Now, due to a very sleazy harbour development project (which is just an excuse to bury toxic waste!), most of the beautiful nature around the town has been bulldozed and the inhabitants are being evicted. There were great parties at Ruigoord all year round, especially on full moons, but their famous and very trippy summer solstice bash was always one of the best. There are still parties going on at the church there (which was spared the wrecking ball), and a Sunday afternoon open stage, but in the future you may need a membership to get in. For news and directions check their web site.

Park Pop - *late June, Zuiderpark, Den Haag*
http://www.parkpop.nl

This has been Europe's biggest free pop festival for more than 20 years, and over three-hundred thousand people usually turn up. Every year sees an interesting line-up of performers playing all kinds of music, but you'll have to truck out to The Hague for this one. Call 0900-340-3505 (ƒ.75/min) or check the website for details.

African Music Festival - *first weekend in August, Delftse Hout, Delft*

Here's another festival that's outside of Amsterdam. This incredible feast of African music gets better every year. Some of Africa's best and most famous stars play here, in a small, wooded area outside of Delft. Tickets are usually ƒ35 (cheaper if you buy in advance). There's camping nearby or hop a train back to Amsterdam - they run all night. Check with the Tourist Office or the Irie Reggae website (see above) for the exact date.

Kwakoe Festival - *mid-July to mid-August, Bijlmerpark, Southeast Amsterdam*
http://www.kwakoe.nl

With over half a million visitors, mostly of Surinamese, Antillean, and Ghanian origin, this is Holland's biggest multicultural festival. It takes place over 6 weekends every summer and admission is free. The biggest draw is the soccer games, but there's also lots of music, food and art. Visit their site or call 697-8821 for details.

Gay Pride Parade - *first weekend in Aug, Amsterdam*

If you're here at the beginning of August make sure to see this fun, extravagant, and somewhat risqué procession of queer-filled boats cruising along the canals. Later in the day there are usually street parties. Call the Gay & Lesbian Switchboard (see Phone Numbers), or stop by Pink Point (see Practical Shit) for information on the route.

Parade - *mid-August, Martin Luther King Park, Amsterdam, 033-465-4577*
http://www.mobilearts.nl

This old-style European carnival is produced by the same trippy people who did the Boulevard of Broken Dreams some years ago. As the sun goes down on the circle of tents, barkers and performers compete to draw you inside, where you'll witness strange, otherworldly spectacles that defy the imagination. It's really something special. Admission is free until about 18:00 and then it's about ƒ7. Once inside, most of the attractions also charge an admission fee, but it's fun just to hang out and people-watch, too.

Uitmarkt - *end of August, central Amsterdam*
http://www.uitmarkt.nl

To celebrate the beginning of the new Dutch cultural season, Amsterdam's streets overflow with theatre, dance, and live music. King Sunny Adé and Dick Dale have both played in recent years. All for free. Check their website for this year's location.

Seven Bridges Jazz Festival - *early September, Reguliersgracht, Amsterdam*
http://www.sevenbridges.nl

Amsterdam's youngest jazz fest is a one day affair that brings together Dutch and international groups. It's a free event that takes place along a canal that's famous for it's seven bridges.

Cannabis Cup Awards - *third week of November, Amsterdam*
http://www.hightimes.com

High Times magazine hosts this annual marijuana harvest festival, and it's getting bigger every year. Several days of cannabis-related events culminate in the actual awards given for the best strains of grass, seed companies, and coffeeshops. It's mainly an American affair. Most of the events cost money, though the Hemp Expo is free and definitely worth a visit.

BARS

Vrankrijk - *Spuistraat 216*
http://www.vrankrijk.org

Even if this long-established squat bar didn't have a sign, you'd have no trouble finding it thanks to the building's wild paint job. Go late if you want to be in a crowd. Buzz to get inside. There you'll find a high-ceilinged room covered with political posters. Despite all the punks hanging around, they play all kinds of music. Occasionally, there are benefits with speakers, bands and videos to raise funds for an organization or a cause. Saturday nights there's dancing in the back room. Every Monday there's a queer night, and the first Friday of the month is for women only. The Vrankrijk is one of the cheapest bars in the city, and any profits are given away to worthy political and social causes. Open: mon-fri 22-2; fri/sat 'til 3. (Map area D5)

Café the Minds - *Spuistraat 245, 623-6784*

This is a comfortably run-down bar with a lot of character. It's located not far from the Vrankrijk. They have a pool table (only ƒ1!), a good pinball machine (5 balls), and they play grunge, rock and metal. It's a fun place to hang out and have a drink while you decide where to go next. Open: daily 21-3. (Map area D5)

De Vaaghuizen - *Nieuwe Nieuwstraat 17, 420-1751*
http://come.to/vaaghuyzen

I've seen several bars come and go at this location, but this one has definitely got it together. They bill themselves as a "before clubbing hangout" and DJs start playing every night at 21:00 - jazz and rare grooves, techno, breakbeats, lounge. The split-level space offers a cosy chill-room upstairs and a bar with a little poolroom down below. It's a very cool little spot. Open: sun 14-1; mon-thurs 17-1; fri 17-3; sat 14-3. (Map area D4)

Café Weber - *Marnixstraat 397, 622-9910*

When you walk in here it looks like a nice, traditional Amsterdam "brown" café. But downstairs you'll find a basement room decked out with old couches, big armchairs, lots of candles and a little greenhouse. It's a great place to sit around and shoot the shit with some friends, even if the beer is a bit overpriced. Its location close to Leidseplein is a plus. Open: sun-thurs 20-3; fri/sat 'til 4. (Map area B7)

Lux - *Marnixstraat 43, 422-1412*

Just a few doors down from Weber, and in the same style, is this funky place. Deejays play here several nights a week, spinning stuff from pop to new wave to drum and bass. Open: sun-thurs 20-3; fri/sat 'til 4. (Map area B7)

De Koe (The Cow) - *Marnixstraat 381, 625-4482*

One block further along you'll find The Cow, which is less trendy than Lux and Weber. It's a pleasant place to escape from the crowds of nearby Leidseplein and hear some blues or rock. In the front you'll find backgammon sets and other games. Downstairs, after 18:00, they serve meals that start at ƒ15. Open: sun 15-1; mon-thurs 16-1; fri/sat 16-3. (Map area B7)

Soundgarden - *Marnixstraat 164-166, 620-2853*

The giant photos of Iggy and Henry in here set the tone for music that's played loud and grungy, much to the appreciation of the leather-clad dudes and chicks that hang here. Actually, a lot of different kinds of people drop in for a night of pool, darts and pinball. Also, the terrace over the canal out back is a great spot to smoke a joint and have a drink in the summer. Open: sun 15-1; mon-fri 13-1; sat 15-3. (Map area B5)

Brouwerij 't IJ - *Funenkade 7, 622-8325*

For those of you who are in town for only a short time, here's your chance to do two tourist essentials at once: drink a Dutch beer other than Heineken and see a windmill. The brewery in this beautiful, old mill sells its delicious draft (with alcohol content up to 9 percent!) to an grateful crowd of regulars in its smoky, noisy pub. On sunny days the terrace is packed, but it's nicer around the corner along the canal. It's a bit out of the centre, not far from the Dappermarkt (see Markets, Shopping chapter) and the Tropenmuseum (see Museums chapter). Open: wed-sun 15-20. (Map area H6)

De Hoogte - *Nieuwe Hoogstraat 2a, 626-0604*

For my dough, this is the best bar along this strip. It's one of the cheapest, too. The good music, relaxed atmosphere, and online computers in the back draw in a cool crowd of all ages. From the window there's a view of the incessant, frenzied bike and pedestrian traffic on the street. It's right next door to The Headshop (see Misc, Shopping chapter). Open: mon-thurs 10-1; fri/sat 10-3; sun 12-1. (Map area E5)

Korsakoff - *Lijnbaansgracht 161, 625-7854*
http://www.korsakoff.nl

The Korsakoff has always been a fun place to dance to punk, grunge, industrial, and the odd tune by Prince, but since their recent extensive renovations it's been a bit unclear what direction they're going in. Traditionally, it's a fairly young crowd that hangs here and whatever happens it'll probably remain a cool place. Buzz to get in. Open: sun-thurs 23-3; fri/sat 'til 4. (Map area B4)

Café Sassoon - *Marnixstraat 79, 420-4075*

Walk into this café/bar at the north end of the Marnixstraat and you can tell immediately that it's an artists' haunt. Paintings, sculptures and other artwork (produced by the regulars) create a cluttered, comfortable environment. Candles add to this relaxing atmosphere and in the back there's usually a couch, some easy chairs and a canal view. During the day they serve cakes and sandwiches from ƒ3.50, and soup of the day for ƒ5. At night, food is available in the restaurant downstairs. On weekends they sometimes have live music and the place gets packed. Open: sun-thurs 15-1; fri/sat 'til 3. (Map area B3)

Getto - *Warmoesstraat 51, 421-5151*

This queer hangout is very different from the famous leather bars that share this strip of the Red Light District. It's a restaurant and bar that's decked out in an arty, comfortable style and it draws a fashionable, mixed crowd. Every second Monday of the month from 21 to 1:00 is the popular women-only club, Getto Girls. And Thursday night bingo gets pretty crowded, too. Getto is open: tues-thurs 16-1; fri/sat 16-1; sun 16-24. (Map area E4)

Lime - *Zeedijk 104, 639-3020*

Whether you're looking for a cool place to hang with a few friends, or just want to have an intimate conversation with someone, this is one of the nicest places to lounge for awhile, especially earlier in the evening before it gets too crowded. The well-designed interior and arty decor make the space feel bigger than it is, and fresh, like the name. Open: tues-sun from 17. (Map area E4)

Time Code - *St Jacobsstraat 17*
http://www.timecode.nl

Being tucked away in a little alley lends this cute bar an underground feel. It's a comfortable place with a good vibe. They show movies on the wall and feature regular DJ nights. As for the drinks, they serve a variety of coffees, energy drinks, and delicious Warsteiner beer - a bit pricey at ƒ4 a pop, but you're paying for the ambience. Open wed,sun 18-1; fri/sat 18-3. (Map area D4)

De Buurvrouw - *St Pieterpoortsteeg 29, 625-9654*
http://www.debuurvrouw.nl

They book lots of acoustic acts here (can't be too noisy cuz of the neighbours), and it's a cool spot to hang out, listen to some music and have a drink. They also host open stage nights for stand-up comedy, poetry and music. Saturdays feature DJs and it gets super busy. If you're on your own, try to leave with a crowd - there's a dark stretch of canal around the corner on Oudezijds Voorburgwal where a few muggings have taken place. Open: sun-thurs 20-3; fri/sat 21-4. (Map area D5)

De Diepte - *St Pieterpoortsteeg 3-5*

Just down the way from De Buurvrouw, in the same tiny alley, look for the sign with the devil and you'll find De Diepte. It's a late-night bar that gets packed in the early hours. Sometimes live bands like The Bones play there, but mostly it's just a noisy crowd enjoying the music ("beat, garage, punk & roll-o-rama") and beer. (Map area D5)

Pompoen - *Spuistraat 2, 521-3000*
http://www.pompoen.nl

The Pompoen is a swank new multi-media centre right in the middle of town. (A far cry from the crazy antics of the Drugs Peace House, which used to be housed in this building!) Five nights a week quality live jazz is performed in the intimate setting of their spacious restaurant/café. There's no cover charge, but when the band comes on they slap an extra ƒ1 onto your drink charge - so your ƒ3.75 cup of coffee becomes ƒ4.75. The food is expensive so I usually just nurse a drink while I soak up the music. Live jazz every Tuesday to Saturday from 21:30. (Map area D3)

De Duivel (The Devil) - *Reguliersdwarsstraat 87, 626-6184*
http://www.deduivel.nl

Years ago, this was the first bar in Amsterdam to play hip-hop on a regular basis. Now their DJs are expanding a bit and throwing in a little funk here, some breakbeats there. Weekends can get really busy. Weeknights are mellower. Peace to all the tourists, cuz I got a lotta love. Open: sun-thurs 20-3; fri/sat 'til 4. (Map area D6)

Du Lac - *Haarlemmerstraat 118, 624-4265*

This place has lots of little rooms and corners to sit in with large or small groups of friends. Their attempt at "zany" decor doesn't quite work, yet it's still a fun, lively place to have a drink. There's a garden in the back and sometimes they feature live music on Sunday afternoons. Open: sun-thurs 16-1; fri/sat 'til 3. (Map area D3)

De Pits - *Bosboom Toussaintstraat 60, 612-0362*

You'd think this bar was any ordinary Dutch drinking spot, what with its with its wood floor, pinball machine, pool table and dartboards. But instead of traditional Dutch sing-alongs, they play punk, hardcore and ska. The owners are friendly and will play requests. You should stop by if you want to know who's playing this sort of music around Amsterdam: there are usually flyers on the bar and sometimes they host gigs there, too. Open: tues-thurs 15-1; fri/sat 15-3; sun 15-1. (Map area A6)

Het Blauwe Theehuis (The Blue Teahouse) - *Vondelpark, 662-0254*
http://www.blauwetheehuis.nl

This circular, spaceship of a building is docked smack-dab in the middle of Vondelpark (see Hanging Out chapter). In the day, especially if it's sunny, the two outdoor terraces are packed with people soaking up the rays. They serve lots of snacks and sandwiches in the ƒ5 to ƒ10 range. At night, the bar upstairs opens and it's a happening little spot with great atmosphere. Sometimes live bands play on Wednesdays.

Saturday is party time with DJs playing anything from disco to motown to hip hop. On Sunday evening things get mellow and you can lounge to jazzy funk, rare grooves and afro-beat. Open: sun-thurs 9-24; fri/sat 9-24 (but if it's busy, they're sometimes open until 3). Note that if you stay real late and the park is deserted when you leave it's best not wander about on your own - however tempting a moonlit stroll might be.

Bar Mono - *Oudezijds Voorburgwal 2, 625-3630*

The best feature of this clean, comfortable bar is its summertime terrace, out beside the canal. Although Mono is right at the edge of the Red Light District, it doesn't have the seedy atmosphere of so many other bars in the area. DJs play on Saturday nights. Open: sun-thurs 11-1; fri/sat 11-3. In winter they open at 17:00. (Map area E4)

Vakzuid - *Olympische Stadion 35, 570-8400*
http://www.vakzuid.nl

The 1928 Olympics were held in Amsterdam and the stadium built for the occasion was recently renovated. The south side houses this restaurant/bar. The food's too expensive for me - actually, so are the drinks at ƒ4.25 for a bottle of juice - but I love the lounge downstairs. With its low, comfortable couches and fake fireplaces, it looks like a 1970's suburban den. And the view of the track and field is awesome. There are DJs on weekends, but for truly relaxed lounging I recommend weekday afternoons when the place is almost empty. In the summer there's a cushy terrace out front - ideal for recovering from the long bike ride out here. Open: mon-thurs 10-1; fri 10-3; sat 12-3; sun 12-1.

Café Saarein - *Elandsstraat 119, 623-4901*

This famous, old-school dyke bar used to be one of the few women-only spaces in town. A couple of years ago it was sold and renovated, and while it remains a gay café, it now caters to a trendier, mixed clientele. The neighbourhood and the building are both pretty and interesting, and it's a pleasant place to stop in for a beer and a game of pool. Open: tues-thurs 17-1; fri/sat 17-2; sun 16-24. (Map area B5)

Azart (Ship of Fools) - KNSM Eiland
http://www.azart.org

I wrote about the bar on this old ship in the very first edition of Get Lost!, before the artists on board sailed away for a tour around the world that lasted years. Now they're back (at least temporarily), and docked in the same old spot on KNSM Eiland (behind the AMP - see Music chapter). The bar opens on Fridays nights around 10, and at 11:00 there's live music, skits, poetry, and anything else the residents dream up during the week. It's a little grungy - the toilet's only for women and guys are expected to pee into the water off the edge of a plank (it feels great!) - but the atmosphere is fun and very welcoming. It's a bit of a trek out here, so you might want to combine it with dinner at End of the World (see Restaurants, Food chapter). Ride your bike or, from Central Station, take bus 32 or 59 (direction KNSM Eiland) or night bus 79 (ask the driver to let you off at Azartplein). (Map area J3)

De Bierkoning (The Beer King) - *Paleisstraat 125, 625-2336*
http://www.bierkoning.nl

It's not a bar, but if you're into beer you'll love this shop which is located just a stone's throw from Dam Square. Wall to wall, ceiling to floor, beer awaits you in bottles of every shape and size. It's all neatly arranged by country, with an entire wall devoted to Belgian brews. If you're flying home from Amsterdam, some of the more exotic beers make great presents. Check out the special offers - free beer mugs with certain purchases, and 10 free beer coasters with every purchase (hey, free is free). The only beer I didn't see here was Duff. Open: mon-13-19; tues-fri 11-19 (thurs 'til 21); sat 11-18; sun 13-17. (Map area D5)

FILM

The great thing about being a visitor to Amsterdam and seeing a movie is that the Dutch never dub films. They are always shown in their original language, with Dutch subtitles. The bad thing about being a visitor to Amsterdam and seeing a movie is the stupid, fucking "pauze" in the middle of most films. Presumably this 15 minute break is a big money-maker for the theatres as everyone files out to buy beer, coffee, and junk food. What it really is though, is an abrupt, unwelcome interruption of the film that never fails to come at the worst moment. Don't say I didn't warn you.

The big first-run theatres are centred mostly around Leidseplein. The City (see below) shows films in the morning on weekends for only ƒ8. Otherwise, prices range from ƒ12.50 to ƒ18.50, with evenings, weekends, and holidays being the most expensive times. The big chains are driving most of the independent theatres out of business, but the few that are still managing to hang on are included in the list below.

For movie listings pick up the Film Agenda, a free weekly listing of what's playing. It's published every Thursday and is available in bars and theatres. Each of the big commercial cinemas also posts a schedule of all the current first-run screenings in Amsterdam near their main entrance. The AUB (see Music chapter) has the schedules of most of the independents, and Shark (see Music again) also lists alternative film events. Online, you can find out what's playing at: *http://www.filmladder.nl.*

THEATRES

Tuschinski - *Reguliersbreestraat 26-28, 626-2633*

This Art Deco theatre opened in 1921 and it might just be the most beautiful movie theatre anywhere. Although it's expensive (ƒ14 up to ƒ18.50), it's worth the price to see a film in the main hall (theatre #1). Occasionally - usually on Sunday mornings - classic silent films are screened with live organ music: quite an impressive spectacle. Go early so you have time to really look at the ornate lobby/café. This is where the queen goes to see movies. (Note: closed for renovations. Re-opening in Nov. 2001) (Map area D6)

Nederlands Film Museum - *Vondelpark 3, 589-1400 ; http://www.filmmuseum.nl*

This museum/cinema/café is situated in a big old mansion in Vondelpark. They screen a couple of different films every day in their two pretty little theatres. The admission price is ƒ12,50 and there's no pauze. You can pick up a monthly listing in the lobby. It's in Dutch, but check where the film was made because they show many from the US (VS) and Britain (GB). Also, some of the foreign films will have a little "eo" listed next to them, which stands for engels ondertiteld - English subtitles. They feature everything from old b+w classics, to rock 'n roll films, to women-in-prison flicks. Every Saturday night in the summer, weather permitting, a big screen is set up outside and a movie is shown for free. (Map area A8)

Film Museum Cinerama - *Marnixstraat 400; http://www.filmmuseum.nl/cinerama*

The film museum now also screens first-run foreign and art films at this theatre near Leidseplein. If you see a film at the Calypso, which has two auditoriums in the same building, make sure you go to the bigger hall - the little one smells like old sweat. (Map area B7)

Filmhuis Cavia - *Van Hallstraat 52-1, 681-1419*
http://www.filmhuiscavia.nl

This little cinema lies just west of the city centre over a boxing club. It seats only about 40 and has an excellent rep programme. They sell cheap beer in their café and admission is a very reasonable ƒ8. Films start at 21:00. Closed in summer. (Map area A2)

Cinema de Balie - *Kleine-Gartmanplantsoen 10, 553-5100*
http:/www.balie.nl

The Balie is a true multimedia centre: film house, café, theatre, digital city, and gallery. They show very cool films, many in English, every Friday, Saturday, and occasionally Sunday nights. They have two theatres, and although the screen isn't very large in the smaller hall, the seats are much more comfortable. De Balie is located just off Leidseplein. Stop in to pick up their schedule (which is in Dutch and English). Admission is ƒ12.50. (Map area C7)

Kriterion - *Roeterstraat 170, 623-1708*
http://www.kriterion.nl

There's always an interesting mix of first-run and classic films being shown on the two screens of this student-run, art-house theatre. There's also a relaxed, busy café in the lobby. The last time I saw a movie here, someone stole my bike from out front. Admission: sun-thurs ƒ12,50; fri/sat ƒ13,50. (Map area F7)

Cinecentre - *Lijnbaansgracht 236, 623-6615*
http://www.cinecenter.nl

On Sundays mornings at 11:00 this multi-plex screens new features for only ƒ7. The rest of the week they charge ƒ10 for matinees, and ƒ15 on evenings and weekends. Most of the films shown here are foreign, so make sure to ask if the subtitles are in English. The Cinecentre is located right across the street from the Melkweg (see Music chapter). (Map area C7)

de Uitkijk - *Prinsengracht 452, 623-7460*
http://www.uitkijk.nl

They show arty first-run stuff here that most of the big theatres ignore, and there's no pauze. Located right by Leidsestraat and next door to Gary's Muffins (see Cafés). Admission: mon-thurs ƒ13; fri-sun ƒ14.50. (Map area C7)

Melkweg Cinema - *Lijnbaansgracht 234-A, 531-8181*
http://www.melkweg.nl

Upstairs at the Melkweg (see Live Venues, Music chapter), there's a cinema that shows interesting retrospectives (for instance, films by Cronenberg, classic porn, or martial arts). There is no pauze. Admission is ƒ12.50 plus ƒ5 for a one-month membership. Films start at 20:00 and on Friday and Saturday there's usually a second screening just after midnight. (Map area C7)

Rialto - *Ceintuurbaan 338, 675-3994*
http://www.rialtofilm.nl

The Rialto is an independent with two theatres. They show some interesting films, but they're mostly foreign, so remember to check the language of the subtitles before you enter. Admission is ƒ10 on Monday, ƒ14 Tuesday to Thursday, and ƒ16 on the weekend. This is also the home of Moviezone (*http://www.moviezone.nl*). If you're 25 or under, you can attend their weekly screenings for only ƒ7. These films are screened every Friday at 15:30 and they show some pretty good stuff. "Grown-ups" pay full price.

Het Ketekhuis - *Haarlemmerweg 8-10, 684-0090*
http://www.ketelhuis.nl

This is the first and only cinema dedicated exclusively to Dutch film. As long as it's Dutch they'll screen it - popular, obscure, shorts, animation, even films made for TV. It's quite unique. The theatre is located on the grounds of the Westergasfabriek (see Music chapter). If this sounds interesting to you, give them a call: some screenings have English subtitles. (Map area A1)

Biotoom 301 - *Overtoom 301, 778-1145*
http://squat.net/overtoom301

This 100-seat cinema is just one of the many cool projects going on in the Academie squat (see Party Venues, Music chapter). Films are shown a couple of days a week and the programming runs from classics to political documentaries to experimental films. To find the theatre, walk to the back of the building and up the stairs. Admission is just ƒ5. (Map area A7)

Tropeninstituut Theater - *Linneausstraat 2, 568-8500*
http://www.kit.nl/tropenmuseum

This theatre, attached to the Tropenmuseum, shows rarely-screened films from all around the world. They're often presented in a series - a month of comedies from Iran, for example. Call to find out if the subtitles are in English (they usually are). Admission: ƒ12.50. (Map area H7)

The Movies - *Haarlemmerdijk 161, 638-6016*
http://www.themovies.nl

There are usually a couple of second-run US or British films playing in the four small halls that make up this theatre, but at ƒ15, the admission ain't cheap. This is the oldest cinema that's still in use in Amsterdam and its little lobby is beautiful. (Map area C2)

Tuschinski Arthouse - *Reguliersbreestraat 34*

Films that used to play at the independent theatres that Pathé drove out of business are now screened here at the Pathé "Arthouse" - at higher admission prices (ƒ14 to ƒ18.50). It's located just a few doors down from the Tuschinski (see above). It's probably very clean and nice.

The City - *Leidseplein, 623-4570*

Totally mainstream, but the giant screen and excellent sound system in theatre #1 are great for movies like *Starship Troopers*. There's an ƒ8 deal on weekend mornings. And no pauze. (Map area C7)

ASCII - *Jodenbreestraat 24 (basement)*
http://www.xs4all.nl/~tank/spg/mumia-nl/plein.htm

Twice a month this internet café (see Hanging Out) turns into Mumiaplein, "a meeting place for film and political discussion". Initiated to make more people aware of the plight of Mumia Abu-Jamal and other political prisoners, they show films and videos that highlight the social, political and economic roots of these injustices. Programming ranges from classics like *12 Angry Men* to modern documentaries about capital punishment in America (a subject more relevant than ever with that moron "dubya" in charge). Mumiaplein happens every 1st and 3rd Thursday of the month starting at 19:30. Admission is free. (Map area E6)

Cineship - *Veemkade (by the Brazilie shopping centre)*

Work on this new, floating cinema should be completed sometime next year. They'll be showing art-films and there are also plans for a restaurant that will have great views over the water.

MISCELLANEOUS FILM STUFF

Amnesty International Film Festival - *626-4436*
http://www.amnesty.nl/filmfestival

The Amnesty International Film Festival is a five-day event focusing on human rights issues. Films and videos (fiction and documentary) are screened at the Balie and City (see above). You'll have to check their site to see when the next one is scheduled.

International Documentary Film Festival - *late November, 627-3329*
http://www.idfa.nl

If you're in town at this time of year, look out for info on this famous festival. It's the biggest of its kind, with over 200 documentary films screened at several theatres around town. Among other places, you can find the programme at the AUB (see music), and De Balie (see above).

Netherlands Film Museum Library - *Vondelstraat 69-71, 589-1435*
http://www.filmmuseum.nl

This library is part of the Netherlands Film Museum (see Film chapter) and lies right at the edge of Vondelpark. It's a bright, airy space, that's perfect for browsing in if you're a film-lover. A large percentage of their 17,000 books are in English and there are over 1,700 magazines, too. Open: tues-fri 10-17; sat 11-17. (Map area A8)

De Filmcorner - *Marnixstraat 263, 624-1974*

This little shop is packed with used videos and films at good prices. Most of it's porno, but they've also got weird shit like super-8 Bruce Lee films and Jerry Lewis movies dubbed into German! Open: mon-fri 9-12 and 13-17:30; sat 9-16. (Map area B4)

The Silver Screen - *Haarlemmerdijk 94, 638-1341*
http://www.silverscreen.nl

New and used books and magazines all about film. Lots of good stuff to browse through here, including posters, cards, videos, and laser discs. Other places with this kind of stuff are Cine-Qua-Non (Staalstraat 14, 625-5588) and, for posters, De Lach (1e Bloemdwarsstraat 14). The Silver Screen is open: mon-fri 13-18; sat 11-18. (Map area C2)

SEX

Sex and lots of it: it's a big part of tourism in Amsterdam. The Red Light District is always crowded and colourful, not to mention sleazy. It's located in the neighbourhood just south-east of Central Station. You'll find streets and alleyways lined with sex shops, live sex theatres, and rows and rows of red lights illuminating the windows of Amsterdam's famous prostitutes. This area is pretty safe, but women on their own sometimes get hassled and may want to tour this part of town during the day. Everyone should watch out for pickpockets.

There's also a smaller Red Light area around Spuistraat and the Singel canal, near Central Station. And another, frequented mainly by Dutch men, runs along Ruysdaelkade by Albert Cuypstraat. But while the Red Light Districts are concentrated in these areas, several of the places I recommend below are in other parts of the city.

In case you were wondering, the services of a prostitute in the Red Light District start at ƒ50 for a blow-job and ƒ50 for a fuck. At that price you get about 15 to 20 minutes. The condom is included free of charge.

SEX SHOPS

You'll find them every twenty metres in the Red Light District and you should definitely take a peek inside one. These places all carry roughly the same selection of sex toys, magazines and videos, ranging from really funny to seriously sexy to disgusting. Remember that videos play on different systems in different parts of the world. If you buy a video, make sure to ask if it will play on your VCR back home. The European system (except for France) is called PAL. North America uses NTSC. Also, most of the cheap stuff is of poor quality: you get what you pay for. For better quality goods I'd recommend the following shop:

Female and Partners - *Spuistraat 100, 620-9152*
http://www.femaleandpartners.nl
This is the coolest and classiest sex shop in Amsterdam. It's women-run and offers an alternative to the very male-dominated sex industry. Inside you'll find a wide range of vibrators, dildos and other sex articles. They're always expanding their selection of books and videos, and they also have some incredibly sexy clothes that you won't find elsewhere. The rubber and leather wear is particularly impressive! Everything in the shop is also available via their very efficient mail-order service. Stop in for info on fetish parties as well. Open: sun/mon 13-18; tues-sat 11-18. (Map C5)

Absolute Danny - *Oudezijds Achterburgwal 78, 421-0915*
http://www.absolutedanny.com
This fetish shop is also woman-run and you can tell the difference from other shops as soon as you walk in. The atmosphere is relaxed and welcoming: single women and couples will feel comfortable shopping here. The owner, Danny, designs a lot of the clothes especially for the shop. She is also co-owner of Demask (Zeedijk 64, 620-5603), the famous fetish-clothing shop. Absolute Danny is open: mon-fri 11-19; sat 11-18; sun 13-18. (Map area E5)

Condomerie Het Gulden Vlies - *Warmoesstraat 141, 627-4174*
http://www.condomerie.com
This was the very first condomerie in the world - and what a selection! There's also an amusing display of condom boxes and wrappers. The laid-back atmosphere here makes the necessary task of buying and using condoms a lot of fun. Open: mon-sat 11-18. (Map area D4)

Nolly's Sexboetiek - *Sarphatipark 99, 673-4757*
In the back of this shop I found a bunch of dusty, straight and gay super 8 and 8mm films from the '60s and '70s for only ƒ7.50. I don't have a projector, but collectors might be interested. Nolly also has a big selection of magazines, some that I didn't see in the Red Light District. Open: mon-fri 10-18; sat 10-17.

Blue and White - *Ceintuurbaan 248, 610-1741*
This is another sex shop that, like Nolly's, is in the neighbourhood of the Albert Cuyp Market (see Markets, Shopping chapter). They've been open for almost 30 years! They have all the required stuff plus a bargain bin full of dildos, other toys, and discount videos. Open: mon-fri 9:30-18 (thurs 'til 21); sat 12-17.

Miranda Sex Videotheek - *Ceintuurbaan 354, 470-8130*
This video store boasts that it stocks over 10,000 videos. Its two floors are loaded with more porno than you can shake a stick at. You'll find just about every kink and perversion you can imagine, and probably some that you can't. Open: daily 10-23.

Alpha Blue - *Nieuwendijk 26, 627-1664*
http://www.crusex.com
Apparently videos are cheaper here than in the nearby Red Light District, but I can't swear by it. They also stock a large selection of magazines. If you don't find what you're looking for, there're 2 more sex shops next door. Open: daily 9-1. (Map D3)

The Bronx - *Kerkstraat 53-55, 623-1548*
This sex shop for gay men has an impressive collection of books, magazines and videos. There are also leather goods, sex toys and the biggest butt-plug I've ever seen! There's a cinema and in the back are some video cabins. If you get really worked up you can run across the street to "Thermos Night" (#58-60; 623-4936; opens at 23:00), where ƒ32.50 (ƒ27.50 if you're under 27) gets you saunas, films, bars, and lots of sweaty guys. Bronx is open: daily 12-24. (Map area C6)

PEEP SHOWS & LIVE SEX

There are several peep show places scattered around the Red Light District. I went into one and this is what I peeped. In a telephone-booth-sized room I put a guilder in a slot and a little window went up. Lo and behold there was a young couple fucking on a revolving platform about two feet from my face. It wasn't very passionate, but they were definitely doing it. One guilder gets you 30 seconds. Then I went into a little sit-down booth and for another guilder I got 100 seconds of a video peep show. There is a built-in control panel with channel changer and a choice of over 150 videos. Everything is there, including bestiality and brown showers. The verdict? Well, I found it kind of interesting in a weird sort of way. There were mostly men peeping, obviously, but there were also some couples looking around. If you're curious, you should go take a look: nobody knows you here anyway.

Peepshow - *Reguliersbreestraat 40* (recently renovated) (Map area D6)
Sex Palace - *Oudezijds Achterburgwal 84* (Map area E5)
Sexyland - *St. Annendwarsstraat 4* (Map area E4)

In the name of research I also saw a few sex shows. At some you can bargain with the doorman, and the average admission price ends up being about ƒ20 to ƒ25. Inside an appropriately sleazy little theatre, women will strip to loud disco music. Sometimes they get someone from the audience to participate by removing lingerie or inserting a vibrator. Then a couple will have sex. It's very mechanical and not very exciting, but it will satisfy your curiosity. At other shows (like Casa Rosso; Oudezijds Achterburgwal 106; 627-8954; *http://www.casarosso.com*) you pay a set price of ƒ50 to sit in a clean, comfortable theatre and watch better-looking strippers and couples. Again, it's not really sexy, but the show was more entertaining. I especially liked one couple who did a choreographed routine to Mozart's Requiem. It was very dramatic and the woman wore lots of leather and had several piercings!

A NOTE ABOUT PROSTITUTION

Because prostitution in the Netherlands has not been forced underground, it is one of the safest places in the world for sex-trade workers and their clients to do business. The status of prostitution in Holland was recently changed from "decriminalized" (subject to pragmatically suspended laws, as with soft drugs) to "legalized" (subject to the same laws as any business).

In spite of this progressive legal climate however, sex-trade workers remain socially stigmatised and are still often exploited. They're required to pay income tax, yet still report having difficultly opening bank accounts or arranging insurance policies if they're honest about the nature of their work. As a result, many of them continue to lead a double life and this is one of the reasons they have such a strong aversion to being photographed. (Don't do it: you're asking for trouble.)

MISCELLANEOUS SEX STUFF

Fetish Parties

Amsterdam is famous for it's fetish parties, where people can dance and socialize in an open manner, as well as enjoy the dungeons, darkrooms, and play areas provided. There's always a strict dress code, (leather, latex, etc). Admission is usually ƒ30 to ƒ50 and often tickets can be purchased in advance. For a listing in English of all the parties around town, go online to Fetish Lights (*http://www.fetishlights.nl*), or pick up flyers at Female and Partners (see above).

Prostitution Information Centre (PIC) - *Enge Kerksteeg 3, 420-7328*
http://www.pic-amsterdam.com

The PIC offers advice and information about prostitution in the Netherlands to tourists, prostitutes, their clients, and anyone else who's interested. It's located in the heart of the Red Light District and is open to the public. Inside you'll find pamphlets, flyers, and books about all aspects of prostitution. They also have a few souvenirs for sale. In the evenings they sometimes host lectures. Closed Sunday and Thursday. Open: tues/wed/fri/sat 11:30-19:30 (possibly longer in the summer). (Map area E4)

Same Place - *Nassaukade 120, 475-1981*
http://www.sameplace.nl

There are lots of sex clubs in Amsterdam, but this one is unique because it bills itself as a Awoman-friendly erotic dance café@, and the cover charge isn=t too expensive. Everyone is welcome: singles, couples, dykes, fags, fetishists, exhibitionists, transsexuals, and anyone else. Entrance is /5 on weeknights and /30 on weekends (which includes /15 worth of drink vouchers). They have piercing and body-painting nights, kinky parties in their cellar (which has a dark-room and S/M corner), and special, women-only parties on the 3rd Sunday of every month. Open: sun/tues-thurs 22-3; fri/sat 22-4. (Map area B4)

Amsterdam Call Girls - *600-2354*
http://www.Amsterdam-Callgirls.com

This fully legal (registered at the chamber of commerce!) escort service is owned and co-operatively run by women. They've been in business for a decade and have an excellent reputation. If you have the money (it's very expensive), and go in for this sort of thing, this is who you should be supporting: women who have taken control of their chosen profession and, as a result, are making their lives and those of their colleagues healthier and safer. Couples are also welcome to call.

DICTIONARY

Note: "g" is pronounced like a low growl, like the noise you make when you try to scratch an itch at the back of your throat, like the ch in Chanukah. I'll use "gh" in my attempt at the phonetic spellings. Good luck (you'll need it).

hello / goodbye = dag (dagh)

see ya = tot ziens (tote zeens)

thank you = dank je wel / bedankt (dahnk ye vel / bidahnkt)

you're welcome / please = alsjeblieft (allsh-yuhbleeft)

fuck off = rot op

do you speak english? = spreekt uw engels? (spreykt oo angles)

how much does that cost? = hoe veel kost dat? (hoo feyl cost dat)

free = gratis (ghrah-tis)

stoned as a shrimp = stoned als een garnaal

got a light? = vuurtje? (foortchye)

rolling paper = vloeitje (flu-ee-chye)

to smoke grass = blow

to blowjob = pijpen (pie-pen)

store = winkel (veenkel)

delicious = lekker

food, to eat, meal = eten (ayten)

rice / noodles = nasi / bami (in Indonesian restaurants)

bon apetit = eet smakelijk (ate sma-ke-lik)

dessert = toetje (too-chye)

cosy = gezellig (ghezeligh)

really? = echt waar? (eght var)

what a drag = wat jammer (vhat yahmmer)

juice = sap

cheers = proost

watch out = pas op

squat = kraak (krahk)

fag = nicht (nickte)

dykes = potten

bicycle = fiets (feets)

left = links (leenks)

right = rechts

asshole! = klootzak! (literally "scrotum" or "ballbag"; kloat-zak)

I practice safe sex = Ik vrij veilig (Ik fry file-igh)

DICTIONARY (continued)

1 =	een (eyn)	
2 =	twee (tvey)	
3 =	drie (dree)	
4 =	vier (feer)	
5 =	vijf (fife)	
6 =	zes (zes)	
7 =	zeven (zeven)	
8 =	acht (ahcht)	
9 =	negen (nayghen)	
10 =	tien (teen)	

1 ounce = 28 grams
1 kilo = 2.2 pounds

Days:

mon =	ma	(maandag)
tues =	di	(dinsdag)
wed =	wo	(woensdag)
thurs =	do	(donderdag)
fri =	vri	(vrijdag)
sat =	za	(zaterdag)
sun =	zo	(zondag)

Temperatures:

°F		°C
104	=	40
95	=	35
86	=	30
77	=	25
68	=	20
59	=	15
50	=	10
41	=	5
32	=	0
23	=	-5
14	=	-10
5	=	-15
-4	=	-20
-13	=	-25

cold = koud (cowd)
hot = heet (hate)
rain = regen (ray-ghen)

Time:

12 noon	12:00
1 pm	13:00
2 pm	14:00
3 pm	15:00
4 pm	16:00
5 pm	17:00
6 pm	18:00
7 pm	19:00
8 pm	20:00
9 pm	21:00
10 pm	22:00
11 pm	23:00
midnight	00:00
1 am	01:00
2 am	02:00
3 am	03:00
etc..	

what time is it? = hoe
laat is het (who laht is het)

 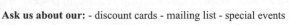

PHONE NUMBERS

EMERGENCY & HEALTH

Emergency: (police, ambulance, fire) 112

Police: (non-emergency; ƒ.30/min) 0900-8844

First Aid: (OLVG Hospital, 1st Oosterparkstraat 179) 599-9111

Sexual Assault Help Line: (mon-fri 10:30-23:00; sat-sun 16-23:00) 613-0245

Crisis Help Line: 675-7575

Anti-Discrimination Office: (complaints about fascism and racism; mon-fri 9-17:00) 638-5551

Doctor Referral Service: (24 hours; ƒ1/min) 0900-503-2042

Health Clinic for the Uninsured: (Gezondheidswinkel De Witte Jas, de Wittenstraat 43-45; mon 12-16:00, 19-20:30; wed/thurs 19-20:30) 688-1140

Women's Health Centre: (free advice and referrals, but no in-house docs; Vrouwengezondheidscentrum Isis, Obiplein 14; mon-fri 10-13:00) 693-4358

Travellers Vaccination Clinic: (GG & GD, Nieuwe Achtergracht 100; mon-fri 8-10:00) 555-5370

Dentist Referral Service: (24 hours; ƒ.45/min) 0900-821-2230

ACTA Dental Clinic: (cheap treatment by students; mon-fri 9-17:00) 518-8888

Pharmacies Info Line: (includes after-hours locations; message is in Dutch) 694-8709

Aids Info Line: (anonymous consultation about aids and safe sex; mon-fri 14-22:00) 0800-022-2220

STD Clinic: (free and anonymous treatment; GG&GD, Groenburgwal 44; mon-fri 8:30-10:30, 13:30-15:30) 555-5822

Birth Control Clinic: (Aletta Jacobshuis, Overtoom 323; by appt. only) 616-6222

Abortion Clinics: (MR'70) 624-5426; (Oosterpark Polikliniek) 693-2151; (PSE) 673-7241; (info line about these and other clinics; mon-fri 9-21:00; ƒ1/min; choose A2" to be connected to an advisor) 0900-9398

Legal Aid Clinic: (mon-fri 9-13:00) 520-5100

GENERAL INFO LINES

Directory Assistance: (*f*2/call) 0900-8008

International Directory Assistance: (*f*1.50/call) 0900-8418

Collect Calls: 0800-0410

Amsterdam Tourist Office (VVV): (*f*1.05/min, which adds up quickly as they often leave you on hold for ages; mon-fri 9-17:00) 0900-400-4040

Public Transport Info: (info on trains, buses & trams throughout Holland; *f*.75/min) 0900-9292

International Train Info & Reservations: (*f*.50/min) 0900-9296

Taxi: 677-7777

Schiphol Airport: (*f*1/min) 0900-0141

Lost and Found Offices: (Amsterdam Police, Stephenstraat 18, near Amstel Station; mon-fri 12:00-15:30) 559-3005; (Central Station, *f*.45/min) 0900-1558; (public transit authority) 460-6060

Lost Credit Cards: (all open 24 hours) Amex 504-8666; Mastercard/Eurocard 030-283-5555; Visa 660-0611; Diners 654-5511

Gay and Lesbian Switchboard: (info and advice; daily 10-22; text phone for the deaf 422-6565; *http://www.switchboard.nl*) 623-6565

Youth Advice Centre: (mon-fri 9-17) 515-8000

Women's Centre: (Vrouwenhuis Amsterdam, Nieuwe Herengracht 95; café open wed/thurs 12-17:00; *http://www.dds.nl/~womenctr*) 625-2066

Weather Forecast: (recorded message in Dutch; *f*1/min) 0900-8003

EMBASSIES & CONSULATES

(070 = Den Haag)

Amerika	575-5309 / 070-310-9209
Australia	070-310-8200
Austria	383-1301 / 070-324-5470
Belgium	070-364-4910
Britain	676-4343 / 070-364-5800
Canada	070-311-1600
Denmark	682-9991 / 070-365-5830
Egypt	070-354-2000
Finland	070-346-9754
France	530-6969 / 070-312-5800
Germany	673-6245 / 070-342-0600
Greece	070-363-8700
Hungary	070-350-0404
Indonesia	070-310-8151
India	070-346-9771
Ireland	070-363-0993
Israel	070-376-0500
Italy	550-2050 / 070-346-9249
Japan	070-346-9544
Luxembourg	310-5622 / 070-360-7516
Morocco	618-1616 / 070-346-9617
New Zealand/Aotearoa	070-346-9324
Norway	624-2331 / 070-311-7611
Poland	070-360-2806
Portugal	070-363-0217
Russia	070-364-6473
South Africa	070-392-4501
Spain	620-3811 / 070-364-3814
Surinam	070-365-0844
Sweden	070-412-0200
Switzerland	664-4231 / 070-364-2831
Thailand	465-1532 / 070-345-9703